A Dream Compels Us
Voices of Salvadoran Women

Edited by
New Americas Press

South End Press
Boston, MA

Editors: **Brenda Carter**
Kevan Insko
David Loeb
Marlene Tobias

Principal Translator: Kevan Insko

Project Coordinators: Brenda Carter
David Loeb

produced by the South End Press collective
manufactured in the USA
Cover by Marlene Tobias
Cover Photo by Adam Kufeld
Photographs by Adam Kufeld (except on pp. 26, 165, 169 by Corinne Dufka, p. 220 by Rick Reinhard, p. 148 by El Salvador Media Project, and p. 128 AMES).

Cataloging-in-Publication Data
A Dream compels us: voices of Salvadoran women / edited by New Americas Press. -- 1st ed.
p. cm.
Bibliography: p.
1. Women--El Salvador--Social conditions. 2. Women--El Salvador--Interviews. I. New Americas Press.
HQ1497.D74 1989
305.42 097284--dc2089-11598
ISBN 0-89608-369-1
ISBN 0-89608-368-3

South End Press, 116 Saint Botolph Street, Boston, MA 02115
98 97 96 95 94 93 92 91 90   2 3 4 5 6 7 8 9

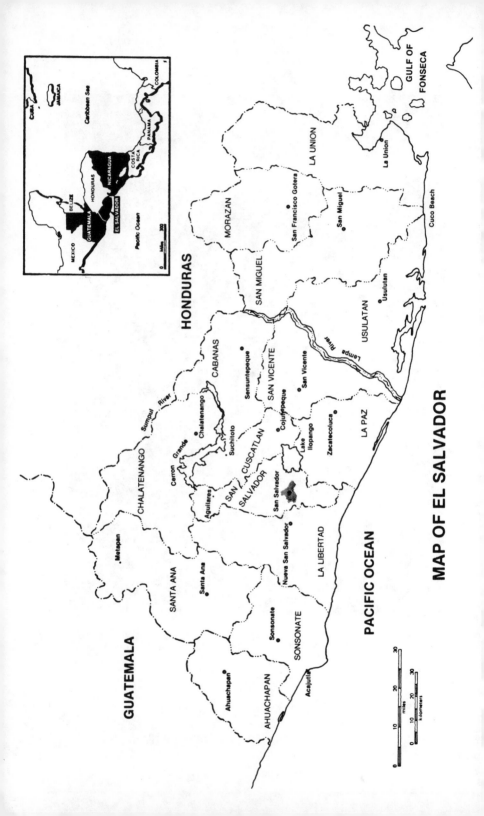

MAP OF EL SALVADOR

Table of Contents

III. "Your People Need You": Women in the FMLN

IV. The Seeds of a New Society: Popular Power in Rural El Salvador

V. "To See Our Homes Again": Salvadoran Women in Exile

Acknowledgements

During the five years that we worked to transform *A Dream Compels Us* from an idea into a book, we were assisted by many wonderful people. Their contributions of time and talent made this book a truly collaborative effort; we could not have brought *A Dream* to light without their help. Because of their invaluable assistance we would like to acknowledge a few of these individuals by name.

Throughout the early stages of the project, Susan Hansell and Gail Enfiajian assisted with transcribing and translating, and Joan Tollifson helped out with the editing. Their work was essential in getting the book off the ground. Stacey Ross handled most of the transcribing and translating towards the end, when fresh energy and an objective perspective were called for.

Beth Wood and Dan Bellm deserve special thanks for their work in researching, conceptualizing and refining the main introduction, while Lisa Robinson, Linda Farthing and Ruth Grabowski helped with the shorter introductory pieces that precede each section.

Laurie Thompson made our work a lot easier by typing out the early versions of the translated interviews. Phil Josselyn provided the computer consulting that allowed us to get everything onto disk and the San Francisco chapter of CISPES generously gave us access to its computer. Floyce Alexander provided copyediting assistance in the project's early stage; at the end, Jean Taylor took on the enormous task of copyediting the final manuscript. Special thanks are due Adam Kufeld for his beautiful photographs and advice on how best to use them. Our gratitude also goes to the patient folks who helped to keep the project going by donating money and purchasing advance copies of the book. And, of course, our deepest appreciaton to New Americas Press for sponsoring and supporting the book all the way up to publication.

1

Finally, and most of all, thanks to the women of El Salvador, whose courage and strength in the face of incredible odds have been an inspiration for us thoughout the process of creating the book. It has been an honor and a privilege to work so closely with their words and thoughts, and it gives us great joy to share them with you, the reader.

The editors,
Brenda Carter
Kevan Insko
David Loeb
Marlene Tobias

Preface

by Grace Paley

I wondered what possible contribution I could make to this rich book of facts, this book of women whose lives have been a longing and a struggle for a revolution that would transform their entire country and include women's lives in that transformation. (This has not always happened in revolutions.)

We were actually on our way to Nicaragua, but stopped in El Salvador. We owed this—the next three days—to our own U.S. government, which did not permit AeroNica to fly from the United States to Nicaragua. Still, the planes of my rich country seem to almost line the skies of the planet—unless some other earth-and-heaven owning nation says, "Not over us! Not just yet!"

In the course of those packed, well-organized days we saw the streets of San Salvador guarded against its own citizens by soldiers dressed in heavy weaponry. We traveled to barbed wire camps, dusty, full of displaced villagers. We learned from the idealistic and endangered Catholic and Lutheran caretakers that the barbed wire was not so much to keep the peasants in as to prevent the death squads from easily snatching a hounded mountain villager or a guerrilla's cousin for questioning and torture.

We saw orphanages where an energetic priest tiptoed around visiting U.S. congressmen. He hoped they would have contacts with philanthropists who might help pay for the cottage camps so that little children could have books to learn from and prostheses to walk with. (Just a few miles from this camp, this orphanage, on the very same road, three nuns and a layworker had been killed, removed from the dangerous occupations of active compassion and prayer by busy killers.) Walking among these children, whose parents were murdered or imprisoned or in exile, I couldn't help but think of Vietnam, where, first, our government created orphans, then decided to adopt, nurture and finally educate them, away from the life and history of their people.

We were able to visit Ilopango Prison—the women's prison—a little while after the fasting, the strikes, some of the struggles described in this collection. And found, ironically, a somewhat freer environment than we had observed in San Salvador. Young women greeted us, black-tammed *comandantes* who had been captured in the mountains. A chorus sang the Internationale to us. A theater group made a play. We met several young women who, having been fruitlessly interrogated, were then shot in the leg to ensure immobility, then raped and arrested. In Ilopango Prison there were many small children—some the babies of love, some of rape. For the legless young women, sixteen-, seventeen-years-old, there was only one pair of crutches, which meant that only one woman could get around at a time, making for a kind of sad listlessness in the others. We called the MADRE[1] office in New York (we were members of a tour organized by MADRE), and they announced this need on WBAI radio station. Within a couple of days the office was jammed with crutches, and within two weeks, a group from NACLA[2] had brought the crutches down to Ilopango. A small shiny pebble in a dirty field of torment, hypocrisy, murder.

Back in San Salvador we visited the Mothers of the Disappeared. Their office had been raided and nearly destroyed a couple of days earlier. The women greeted us generously, as though they didn't know that it was our U.S. tax money that was being used to increase and deepen their sorrow. (They knew a great deal.) They had placed two huge photograph albums on the table which we looked at. We could hardly turn the pages as it would be an act of abandonment of the murdered son or daughter photographed on that page—usually a teacher or health worker, the same dangerous professions attacked by the Contras in Nicaragua.

In San Salvador I.

Come   look   they said
here are the photograph albums
these are our children.

We are called the Mothers of the Disappeared
we are also the mothers of those who were seen once more
and then photographed   sometimes parts of them
could not be found

a breast   an eye   an arm is missing
sometimes a whole stomach
that is why we are called   The Mothers
of the Disappeared   although we have these large
heavy photograph albums full of beautiful
torn faces

In San Salvador II.

Then one woman spoke About my son
she said   I want to tell you   This
is what happened

    I heard a cry   Mother
mother   keep the door closed   a scream
the high voice of my son   his scream
jumped into my belly   his voice
boiled there and boiled until hot water
ran down my thigh

    The following week I waited
by the fire making tortilla   I heard What?
the voice of my second son   Mother quickly
turn your back to the door   turn your back
to the window

    And one day of the third week
my third son called me   oh mother please
hurry up   hold out your apron   they are
stealing my eyes

    And then in the fourth week my
fourth son   No

  No   It was morning   he stood
in the doorway   he was taken right
there   before my eyes the parts of
the body of my son were tormented   are
you listening? do you understand
this story? there was only one
child   one boy   like Mary I had
only one son

I have written these few remembrances of a country my country won't leave alone because the faces of the people I saw in those short days do not leave me. I see it clearly right now. The teachers of ANDES—the teachers' union—demonstrating on the steps of the great Cathedral, where hundreds, mourning Oscar Romero's murder, had been shot, only a couple of years earlier. They held banners and called for decent wages, and an end to disappearances. On those historic steps they seemed naked to the rage of the death squads. I could see how brave they were because their faces were pale and their eyes, searching the quiet crowd, were afraid. Still, they stood there, shouted the demands, and would not be moved.

Grace Paley
November 1988

Members of COMADRES occupying the Metropolitan Cathedral in San Salvador to protest government human rights violations (May 1986).

Introduction

The lives of Salvadoran women have never been easy. In one of the poorest countries of Latin America, they haul water, work on small, rocky plots of land or in rich people's homes, and struggle, often alone, to raise their malnourished children. Since the mid-1970s, when violence by the Salvadoran army and by paramilitary "death squads" turned a political conflict into a bloodbath, hardship has turned into terror and grief. Yet out of this nightmare, a spirit of resistance has been reborn in the women of El Salvador, nurtured by the dream of a new nation.

Statistics merely hint at what the people of El Salvador have endured. Since 1979, nearly 70,000 Salvadorans have died in politically related violence. More than 7,000 others have disappeared. Well over one million have been displaced from their homes by the conflict: over 800,000 have fled the country and over 600,000 are displaced within El Salvador. All this in a country with a population of 5,200,000—slightly less than that of the state of Massachusetts.

Although intense poverty and political repression have long prevented many Central Americans from taking action toward social change, El Salvador has a long tradition of popular rebellion and defiance. Women, such as those who speak in *A Dream Compels Us,* have come together at great risk to build better lives for themselves, for their children and for all Salvadorans. They have organized neighborhood committees to confront the basic issues of survival—the lack of water and electricity, the scarcity and high cost of food, the lack of jobs in a nation with a combined unemployment/underemployment rate of over 70 percent. They have taken leadership roles in human rights organizations and in the trade union movement. In the countryside and in refugee communities they have organized literacy classes, production workshops, health campaigns and childcare centers. And they have created women's organizations to nurture and focus their strength and commitment.

It is in this context that we present *A Dream Compels Us*. Our aim has been to give Salvadoran women a forum to explain in their own words the process of profound social transformation occurring in El Salvador. The pieces in this book cover the period from 1980 to 1988, depicting the development of a broad revolutionary movement and women's participation in it over the course of a decade.

A Dream Compels Us is not an academic study of an interesting but peripheral aspect of a Third World revolution. The massive incorporation of women into the political process in El Salvador has profound implications both for El Salvador's revolution and for women's liberation throughout the world. Salvadoran revolutionaries have long understood the importance of incorporating women into the movement and have encouraged the development of separate women's organizations for that purpose. This has enabled large numbers of women to break through the traditional obstacles to activism. Grassroots organizing and political participation have had far-reaching effects on women's everyday lives, opening the possibility of redefining their roles as women in society and in the home.

Since 1987, Salvadoran women's groups have achieved an unprecedented breadth within the resurgent popular opposition movement. Yet these groups do not characterize themselves as a "women's movement," nor do the women involved describe themselves as "feminists," a term which in El Salvador suggests a view of women's liberation as being separate from the challenge of transforming society as a whole. The priorities of these groups are national: an end to hunger, misery, repression and war. Women's concerns, however, are not being deferred to some distant future; even in the midst of the current national crisis, women's organizations are raising issues such as employment discrimination, female sexuality, domestic violence and the sexual abuse of children.

Of course, the nature of women's organizing in El Salvador has not evolved in isolation from the rest of the world. Struggles and ideas advanced within the international women's movement find their reflections in El Salvador. Women from Africa, Asia and Latin America have been working to redefine the western conception of feminism within the context of their countries' needs to be free of foreign domination, distorted economic development, hunger and war. These women contend that such issues are the proper concern and focus of women's movements, since they define the conditions of women's lives throughout much of the world. Yet the question still remains: if women place broad political and social issues at the top of their own agendas, will issues specific to women take a back seat once a popular revolutionary victory is achieved?

Experiences in various Third World revolutions, as well as in more "developed" socialist societies, indicate that this is not merely a theoretical question. While Salvadoran women do not claim to have a definitive answer, it is worthwhile to examine their experience as an advance in the global process of human liberation. At the very least, the Salvadoran revolutionary experience cannot be understood without hearing from the women who are helping to shape it. According to the Women's Association of El Salvador (AMES), one of the most influential women's organizations of the 1970s and 1980s:

> The revolutionary process can be measured by observing the extent of women's participation...It is impossible to speak of a true revolution if women continue to be subjugated and marginalized. In a true revolution, there are advances by women in all areas...The revolutionary process that is now in progress in our country has as one of its goals the abolition of social inequality. As a result, the equality of women in all aspects of society is a primary objective.[3]

The inextricable bond between the two broad objectives of political revolution and social transformation underlies the words and deeds of every woman who speaks from the following pages.

In *A Dream Compels Us,* the reader will hear a wide range of voices, from the uneducated peasant to the sophisticated theoretician, from the high-ranking to the rank-and-file, from those who fight with the guerrillas in the mountains to those who confront government security forces in city streets, from those who have had to flee their country to those who have stayed to fight.

The book is divided into five sections, each of which covers one of the principal areas of activity through which women have become involved. "We Have Found the Strength" focuses on women's participation in the broad-based popular movement that flourished in the 1970s and has been painstakingly rebuilt in the late 1980s. "With One Single Voice" explores the history of organizations formed specifically to bring women into social activism and to address their needs. "Women in the FMLN" discusses the impressive incorporation of women into the political and military structures of the armed revolutionary movement, the Farabundo Martí National Liberation Front. "Popular Power in the Countryside" looks at the role women have played in building new democratic communities and institutions in areas wrested from government domination. Finally, "To See Our Homes Again" introduces representatives of that one-quarter of the Salvadoran population who, although displaced from their homes by war, have never given up the dream of rebuilding their homes and their country. The five sections combine interviews, essays, testimonies and other forms of expression to provide a view of a process of change that is both expressly political and deeply personal.

A Brief History

The Pipil Indians who migrated south from Mexico to El Salvador many centuries ago established a communal, agricultural way of life which remained unchanged until the Spanish conquest under Pedro de Alvarado in 1524. Within 50 years, violence and disease reduced the indigenous population from 500,000 to 75,000. Three centuries of Spanish rule created the export-dependent economy and the disparity between rich and poor that remain defining characteristics of the country to this day.

Women were active in the uprisings of 1811 and 1814 which led to El Salvador's independence from Spain in 1821. But independence brought few changes; Indian peasants continued to work mainly on communal lands to produce indigo and cocoa for export to Great Britain, El Salvador's main trading partner. A major Indian uprising in 1833 was crushed by the new rulers of independent El Salvador, who proved to be no less ruthless than their former Spanish masters.

By the late 19th century, coffee had become king in El Salvador—accounting for 95 percent of export earnings—and U.S. interests were surpassing those of the British. In order to create a mobile wage-labor force and to free up land for large coffee plantations, the government began breaking up the Indians' communal lands, by force when necessary, finally abolishing them altogether in 1881. In the cities, the poor earned miserably low wages as maids, gardeners, factory workers and prostitutes.

The *Matanza*

By the 1920s, peasants and city dwellers were organizing to seek change through electoral politics and peaceful demonstrations. In December 1922, a women's march through the center of the capital was fired upon by the army, and dozens of women died. In 1932, the military regime of General Maximiliano Hernández Martínez nullified the national election in which the Communist Party of El Salvador, led by Agustín Farabundo Martí, had won several key government posts. In response, the Party and other peasant and Indian groups planned a coordinated workers' revolt and peasant uprising. The plan was discovered by the government and Martí was arrested, but due to poor communication, the peasants went ahead with the uprising. The military regime's response was swift and brutal. Martí and many of his colleagues were executed, and over 30,000 other Salvadorans, most of them Indians, were massacred within three weeks. Armed mainly with machetes, the rebels were unable to defend themselves against the government's armed forces. Historian Thomas P. Anderson, who interviewed survivors of the *matanza* (massacre), wrote, "The extermination was so great that they could not be buried fast enough, and a great stench of rotting flesh permeated the air of western El Salvador."[4] Survivors abandoned their indigenous language, dress and culture, and few cries of protest about the conditions of the poor were heard for another three decades. The government tried to purge all documentation of the *matanza,* but the outrage is indelibly marked in the national consciousness. The 1932 uprising and massacre demonstrate that El Salvador's conflict is deeply rooted in the country's internal conditions, traceable to a time long before revolution came to Cuba and Nicaragua.

The Movement Reawakens

After the *matanza* the tightly knit oligarchy of large landowners strengthened their control of the coffee economy, supported by a fifty-year series of military governments. Called *Los Catorce,* or the "Fourteen Families," this group intermarried, conducted business together, sent their children to schools in the United States and Europe, spent fortunes on imported luxuries and ruled El Salvador with an iron hand. By the 1970s, this wealthiest 2 percent of the Salvadoran population owned 60 percent of the land—in a country where 60 percent of the people still live in rural areas, dependent on the land for survival.

By the 1960s this coffee elite had diversified into banking, insurance and industry, but the transition to an industrialized economy, encouraged by President Kennedy's Alliance for Progress, did nothing to change the power structure of the country. Poverty, in fact, was intensifying. Despite a 24 percent growth spurt in manufacturing in the 1960s, the average manufacturing and service sector wage was $1.64 a day in 1973. Between 1961 and 1975, the proportion of landless peasants grew from 11 percent to 40 percent.

Many observers consider the 1972 presidential election the turning point after which armed revolution became inevitable. The Christian Democratic Party had formed a coalition with two leftist parties to run

José Napoleón Duarte, the mayor of San Salvador, as their candidate for president, and Guillermo Ungo of the National Revolutionary Movement for vice president. When early returns appeared to favor Duarte and Ungo, the government stopped announcing the count and declared victory for the military candidate. Duarte was arrested by the army, beaten and forced into exile.

After the stolen election of 1972, many people gave up hope that the government would ever respond positively to their legitimate demands and they began to seek out radical alternatives. Workers, peasants, women, students and shantytown dwellers all began to develop their own organizations to demand basic political and economic rights. While the demands were not new, the extent of the organizing was. By 1979, major demonstrations in San Salvador were drawing as many as 250,000 people. At the same time, the Sandinista victory against the Somoza regime in neighboring Nicaragua demonstrated that revolutionary change was indeed possible in Central America. Many of the women we will meet in *A Dream Compels Us* trace their involvement in political activity to this period of extraordinary ferment.

A new spirit of activism was also emerging within the Catholic Church following the Second Vatican Council and the 1968 conference of Latin American bishops in Medellín, Colombia. Peasants and church workers formed Christian "base communities" and agricultural cooperatives throughout rural El Salvador in the late 1960s and early 1970s. Progressive young priests organized study sessions in which peasants reflected on local conditions in light of biblical texts. Traditional fatalism gave way to the view that poverty and repression were less a matter of God's will than of human injustice. Many rural women who had never imagined a political role for themselves joined the massive outcry for land reform, motivated above all by a religious faith that justice could prevail on earth.

On the Brink of Revolution

The military government's response to this political awakening was soon evident: mutilated bodies appeared on roadsides and in clandestine graveyards with numbing frequency. White handprints appeared on doorways, the chilling signature of "death squads" organized by the military and the oligarchy to murder outspoken activists and their families—often in broad daylight.

Convinced that open, "legal" political organizing would only lead to the cemetery, not to significant change, small numbers of political activists began organizing the clandestine guerrilla units that would later form the nuclei of the Farabundo Martí National Liberation Front (FMLN). While their armed activities throughout the 1970s remained on a small scale, by 1979 these groups had grown enough to be perceived as a serious threat by the military regime.

In 1979, fearing that El Salvador would soon undergo a revolution similar to Nicaragua's, a group of young military officers staged a coup against the notoriously corrupt regime of General Carlos Humberto Romero. They formed a government which included civilians from a wide spectrum of political parties and announced a series of reforms to address the demands of the popular movement. But most of the civilian cabinet ministers resigned in January 1980, frustrated by the obstruction of meaningful changes by the military and the oligarchy. Three more juntas followed—headed after March 1980 by José Napoleón Duarte as president—but each in succession seemed less able to implement promised reforms or halt human rights atrocities. Between 1979 and 1981, some 34,000 politically motivated killings occurred in El Salvador.

Meanwhile, in 1980 and 1981, the Salvadoran government received over $210 million in military and economic aid from the United States, which had become deeply committed to thwarting a second revolution in Central America. The junta combined mild reforms with severe repression against those calling for more fundamental change; its most heralded measure was the U.S.-designed "Land to the Tiller" agrarian reform program, modeled after a plan carried out in Vietnam in 1968. Between 1980 and 1985, the United States channeled $250 million into the program in an effort to pacify an increasingly organized and angry rural population and to win their "hearts and minds" away from the revolutionary movement.

But for the landless families who had seen hope in the agrarian reform, the plan was at best a disappointment. Most of the plots distributed were too small and infertile to sustain a family, and credit and technical assistance were unavailable; many peasants found themselves in debt for up to thirty years to pay for useless land. Worst of all, the army used the lure of agrarian reform to identify and murder peasant leaders, many of them from the Christian base community movement.

By 1979, the Archbishop of San Salvador, Monsignor Oscar Romero, had become the military government's most forceful and fearless critic, speaking out in defense of the poor and even appealing to President Jimmy Carter to halt military aid to the junta. On March 24, 1980, one day after calling upon the soldiers of the National Guard to disobey the orders of their superiors, Romero was assassinated while saying mass. Several days later, as thousands of people gathered for his funeral outside the National Cathedral, gunfire rang out from the government building next door; twenty-six mourners were killed as the crowd surged into the Cathedral to seek refuge. Archbishop Romero is now revered as a martyr; as a powerful symbol for the popular movement of El Salvador, his image is displayed prominently in many protest activities.

The year 1980 was marked by many acts of terrible violence. In May, some 600 Salvadoran peasants were massacred while fleeing across the Honduran border at the Sumpul River, shot at by Salvadoran troops on one side of the river and by Honduran troops on the other. In June, the army stormed the University of El Salvador campus, killing at least fifty people. On December 2, four U.S. churchwomen were raped, killed and left in a shallow grave near the capital. Forced to respond to these murders of North Americans, the Carter administration stopped U.S. economic aid for a mere two weeks, and military assistance for a month.

The Opposition Organizes

Shortly after Archbishop Romero's death, many civilian opposition groups—including union federations, peasant groups, political parties and the women's group AMES—formed the Democratic Revolutionary Front (FDR) to coordinate the popular mass movement and present a political alternative to the junta. But the military would not tolerate a united opposition. In November 1980, FDR President Enrique Alvarez and five other FDR leaders were kidnapped, tortured and executed by government security forces; Guillermo Ungo, Duarte's 1972 running mate, succeeded Alvarez as head of the opposition alliance. But the repressive conditions made it impossible for the FDR to function openly inside El Salvador. Most of the popular organizations disbanded or moved into the zones of rebel control, while the political parties initiated diplomatic work outside the country to build support for the opposition movement and a political solution to the conflict.

The five revolutionary parties which had initiated armed activities in opposition to the regime during the previous decade also united in 1980 to form the FMLN. Since then, the FMLN has developed a seasoned guerrilla army and a coordinated political structure capable of controlling significant portions of the countryside. It is the primary political opposition force in El Salvador, working in an alliance with the FDR to provide a revolutionary alternative to the current regime and to reach a negotiated political settlement to the conflict.

Women have been active at all levels of the FMLN since its inception. The original leadership of the FMLN included two women: Melida Anaya Montes, killed in an internal dispute in 1983, and Ana Guadalupe Martínez, now a representative of the Political and Diplomatic Commission of the FMLN/FDR. Current estimates indicate that over one third of the FMLN's active forces are women, including an all-women's battalion formed in the early 1980s.

A State of War

During 1981, the FMLN made significant military gains, especially in the northern countryside, but a major insurrection in January did not lead to a hoped-for revolutionary victory. The guerrilla offensive also coincided with the beginning of Ronald Reagan's hard-line administration in Washington. The "Reagan Doctrine" committed the U.S. government to halting and rolling back the "spread of communism" throughout the world, but especially in Central America, its "backyard." In El Salvador, vowed Secretary of State Alexander Haig, the United States was going to "draw the line."

El Salvador held a national election in March 1982 to demonstrate a supposed return to democracy. On the evening news in the United States, images of mutilated bodies gave way to pictures of long lines of enthusiastic voters. But Salvadorans turned out *en masse* largely to receive a stamp on their *cédulas* (ID cards), which were essential for receiving paychecks or hospital care and were frequently demanded at military checkpoints. Without a stamp to show they had voted, civilians could be detained as "subversives," even tortured or killed.

The FMLN/FDR rejected the elections as a "puppet show," but since "democracy" had certifiably returned to El Salvador, U.S. congressional opposition evaporated, and economic and military aid to the Salvadoran government soared. In 1982, U.S. aid amounted to $264.2 million; in 1986, it totaled $625.4 million—over $1.5 million per day. By 1988, it exceeded the Salvadoran government's contribution to its own budget. Military aid paid for training of the Salvadoran army and police, and provided them with highly sophisticated weaponry. U.S. aid also financed the so-called "low-intensity war" of invasions and bombings in the extensive rural areas where the FMLN had achieved a large degree of operational control.

In the countryside, especially in the northern and eastern provinces of Chalatenango, Cuscatlán, Cabañas and Morazán, a system of dual power had begun to develop. As the government lost its grip on these areas, many peasants lent their political and material support to the guerrilla cause, and developed self-sufficient local governments and services, such as schools, clinics, women's groups and networks to produce and distribute food. Despite heavy attacks on these "zones of popular control," the FMLN survived and grew. On the other hand, despite an enormous infusion of U.S. aid, the army failed to gain the upper hand in the conflict. It had new helicopters and sophisticated intelligence equipment, but it could overcome neither the low morale within its ranks nor the mistrust of a terrorized population, thousands of whom were fleeing to Honduras, Mexico and the United States. With neither side able to win a military victory, the war intensified, and dragged on.

The Duarte Government and the Opposition

War-weariness was a major reason for the presidential election victory of José Napoleón Duarte in June 1984. Duarte defeated Roberto D'Aubuisson of the right-wing ARENA (Nationalist Republican Alliance) Party—a man widely believed to have founded the death squads and to have ordered the murder of Archbishop Romero—by pledging to settle the civil war, curb and prosecute army abuses, resume land redistribution and institute other economic reforms.

But Duarte failed to maintain his hold on popular support for long. Not a single army officer was prosecuted; agrarian reform came to a halt; the stepped-up war continued to displace thousands of people; and the government continued to stifle dissent through arbitrary arrests and torture. Yet it was also in this period that the popular movement began to revive itself, wedging a foot in the crack in the door created by Duarte's campaign promises of a "democratic opening." The first groups to demonstrate publicly were human rights organizations such as COM-ADRES (the Committee of Mothers of Political Prisoners, the Disappeared and the Assassinated of El Salvador). Through the worst of the repression, these predominantly female groups had continued to document the murders, tortures and disappearances of civilians. The example of these courageous women marching down the streets in black dresses and white scarves, carrying photos of their murdered or missing relatives, was instrumental in reasserting the possibility of protest and in encouraging the resurrection of the popular opposition movement.

As the war wrecked the economy, Duarte's promises to increase wages and expand social services turned into calls for austerity and more sacrifice. Rather than negotiating seriously with the FMLN, Duarte demanded that they disarm and join the "democratic" process. Rather than seeking democracy or an end to the war, Duarte pursued a military victory—through a Vietnam War-style "scorched earth" policy which killed far more civilians than rebels.

By early 1986, aerial bombardment and large-scale army operations had made life in most of the peasant communities in FMLN-controlled zones impossible to maintain. Many *campesinos* were captured by the armed forces and taken to refugee camps around San Salvador. Many others fled to makeshift cardboard and tin barrios that sprang up around the capital and other urban areas. Separated from their livelihood on the land and unable to find employment in a collapsing economy, most of the displaced have had to rely on meager handouts from church charities to survive.

On the morning of October 10, 1986, an earthquake measuring 7.5 on the Richter scale struck the heart of San Salvador. When the tremors stopped, 1,500 people were dead, 30,000 injured and 200,000 homeless. In the following weeks and months, anger grew as the Duarte government and the army did little to help the poorest victims, concentrating instead on tearing down damaged structures and standing guard to prevent looting. The already weakened government was now widely charged with corruption, including the outright theft of millions of dollars in international aid.

The Current Situation

Since 1985, disillusionment with Duarte—even among his former supporters—has helped fuel an impressive resurgence of the popular opposition movement in San Salvador and throughout the country. On May Day, 1986, 100,000 people marched through the capital, calling for peace talks between the government and the FMLN, for an end to bombing and U.S. military aid and for economic justice. That demonstration was called by a newly formed coalition of independent trade unions and other groups, the National Unity of Salvadoran Workers (UNTS), the largest popular coalition since 1980. By 1986, labor strikes, increasing in size and militancy, became the central focus of the legal opposition and in 1988 the UNTS identified women workers as its highest organizing priority.

Women, in fact, are organizing as never before to protest the destruction of their families, the deterioration of their standard of living and the continuation of the war. The most striking development is the proliferation of small committees of women in poor communities, in unions and in popular organizations. In early 1986 there were no public organizations representing women in government-controlled areas. But by 1988, there were dozens of groups with the prefix "COFE" (standing for *comisión feminina,* or women's committee), such as COFESTISSS (the women's committee of STISSS, the hospital workers' union) and COFEDYDES (the women's committee of CODYDES, the organization of unemployed workers). Women in many poor rural communities have also formed their own committees, as have women in the shantytowns in and around San Salvador.

While most of these committees are quite small, they generally participate in one of the women's coordinating committees or associations that have formed since 1987. (By late 1988, there were five such associations.) These larger groups, in turn, help to organize new grassroots committees and to provide a political framework linking these efforts with the overall popular movement for peace and justice. They organize demonstrations, such as the 1988 International Women's Day marches in San Miguel and San Salvador that each drew between 1,000 and 1,500 women. They also organize forums that bring together women from all across the country. Through these efforts, thousands of previously unorganized women are being mobilized to protest the government that has made it impossible for them to sustain their families. Much more so than in the early 1980s, women are a visible and integral part of a massive opposition movement.

As this broad-based movement has grown, so has the threat of violence against it. Repression directed against opposition groups and their members has increased dramatically since 1987. Actions such as the bombing of offices of popular movement groups (FECMAFAM in May 1987, the UNTS in April 1988, Federation of Salvadoran Workers in February 1989) are clearly intended to discourage protests.

The military high command has openly expressed its displeasure at the growing numbers of militant demonstrations organized by workers, students, women, the displaced and *campesinos;* security forces are once again attacking such protests and abducting opposition leaders. In July 1988, twenty marchers were wounded when police opened fire on a peaceful UNTS demonstration that was demanding the release of a detained union leader. In January 1989 troops of the 1st Infantry Brigade fired on a demonstration of 150 women from a poor barrio of San Salvador who were protesting the forced recruitment of their teenage sons into the Salvadoran army.

Death squad activity has also soared since late 1987, beginning with the assassination of Herbert Anaya, president of the non-governmental Human Right Commission (CDHES). The commission documented 1,832 such political killings and 231 additional unsolved disappearances in 1988. In April 1989, a leading member of the National Coordinating Committee of Salvadoran Women (CONAMUS), Cristina Gomez, was abducted and murdered by unidentified armed men believed to be from the nearby air force base. As in the early 1980s, the government has done nothing to identify and punish those responsible for these crimes. Because, in fact, all of these acts of repression, whether carried out by men in uniform or street clothes, are part of the government's policy to silence the popular movement and are directed by the government's security forces.

Choices for the Future

As of this writing, the war goes on. While the Peace Accords signed by the five Central American presidents at Esquipulas, Guatemala in August 1987 raised hopes that peace might be on the horizon, any possible progress towards a negotiated political settlement in El Salvador has been blocked by the intransigence of the U.S. government and the Salvadoran military. In January 1989, the FMLN made a dramatic new offer to accept the results of forthcoming elections conducted by the government, provided that all Salvadorans (including refugees and residents of zones of rebel control) be allowed to vote; that guarantees against government fraud and military intimidation be instituted; and that the vote be postponed six months to implement these conditions. The proposal received widespread support from the population, including the four major labor federations, the organizations of the popular movement, the Church hierarchy, professionals and many of the political parties. However, the offer was spurned by Duarte, ARENA and the military high command. And so a promising opportunity for peace was lost, and the March 1989 presidential elections proceeded as scheduled. The elections were won by ARENA's Alfredo Cristiani, a wealthy, U.S.-educated coffee grower with family and business ties to El Salvador's traditional elite.

While Cristiani is being portrayed as a "moderate" by a Bush administration anxious not to lose Congressional support for continued aid to El Salvador, ARENA's victories in both the municipal and national elections of 1988 and 1989 spell trouble for the United States's counter-insurgency strategy. The goal of the strategy has been to create a "democratic center" to win over a portion of the guerrillas' social base. However, with the erosion of Duarte's health and credibility and the defeat of his party, the United States is left without a suitable vehicle for its strategy. Unlike the Christian Democrats, ARENA makes no promises to accomodate the economic and social needs of the population. In fact, ARENA leaders have warned that popular protests and strikes will be met with military force. Moreover, Roberto D'Aubuisson, who retains control of the party he founded, has criticized both Duarte and Washington for tying the hands of the military and promises a "total war" against the FMLN and its supporters.

A social explosion in El Salvador now seems inevitable. Instead of accepting the FMLN's offer to negotiate an end to the conflict and broaden the political process, the Salvadoran government has opted to intensify its war against the Salvadoran people—a war that will be kept alive by massive infusions of U.S. aid. For even as it loses its grip on events in El Salvador, Washington continues to funnel over $1 million a day (over $718 million in FY1987-88) to the government in San Salvador.

With the rise of ARENA on one hand and the resurgent popular movement and FMLN/FDR on the other, the U.S. government and the American public are presented with a clear choice in El Salvador. We can continue to bankroll a government which is now in the hands of an extreme right-wing party that promises to solve the country's problems through increased bloodshed. Or we can heed the broad-based popular movement's plea for an end to U.S. interference, and for a national dialogue, involving *all* sectors of Salvadoran society. Every day of U.S. funding, every day of delay, means more bodies to bury, more wounds to heal, more homes to rebuild.

While the collapse of the old order in El Salvador appears more certain every day, the work to build a new and more just society will confront the Salvadoran people with enormous tasks for years to come. But hearing the stories of Salvadoran women inspires confidence that the obstacles are surmountable. We have gathered together the voices of many of these women in *A Dream Compels Us,* and we invite you to share their faith, their pain and their dream.

April 1989

Glossary

ADEMUSA *Asociación de Mujeres Salvadoreñas*/Association of Salvadoran Women: Organization of independent women activists, based in San Salvador, founded in 1987. Member organization of COPROUMSA (see below).

AMS *Asociación de Mujeres Salvadoreñas*/Association of Salvadoran Women: Organization of women from the countryside and small towns in southeastern El Salvador (San Miguel, San Vicente, Usulután, Morazán), founded in 1987.

AMES *Asociación de Mujeres de El Salvador*/Women's Association of El Salvador: Organization of women active in the popular and revolutionary movements, founded in 1978. Associated with the Popular Liberation Forces (FPL) and the Popular Revolutionary Bloc (BPR). After 1981, AMES worked extensively with women in rural zones of popular control. Became part of Salvadoran Women's Union (UMS) in 1987.

AMPES *Asociación de Mujeres Progresistas de El Salvador*/Progressive Women's Association of El Salvador: Organization of women founded in 1975, associated with the Salvadoran Communist Party (PCS). Became part of UMS in 1987.

ANDES *Asociación Nacional de Educadores Salvadoreños "21 de junio"*/National Association of Salvadoran Educators "21st of June": Progresssive independent union of public school teachers, founded in 1965, and active in popular movement throughout the 1970s and 1980s.

BPR *Bloque Popular Revolucionario ("Bloque")*/Popular Revolutionary Bloc: Large coalition, or front, composed of numerous popular sector organizations, including students, peasants, workers and slum dwellers. Active throughout the late 1970s, it was one of the founding organizations of the Democratic Revolutionary Front (FDR).

campesino/a: peasant

CDHES *Comisión de Derechos Humanos de El Salvador*/Human Rights Commission of El Salvador: Non-governmental organization that documents and protests human rights violations and abuses, founded in 1978.

Christian base community (CBC): Group of people organized on basis of religious faith, for the dual purposes of religious reflection and social action. Base communities were started in the late 1960s and early

1970s by Catholic priests and lay workers influenced by liberation theology.

CNR *Coordinadora Nacional de Repoblación*/National Coordinating Committee for Repopulation: Founded in 1986 by groups of people displaced by the war, to promote and coordinate their efforts to return and repopulate their villages in the countryside.

colón: Salvadoran unit of currency. Standard exchange rate in 1988 was five colones to one U.S. dollar.

COMADRES *Comité de Madres de los Presos Políticos, los Desaparecidos y los Asesinados "Monseñor Oscar Romero"*/Committee of Mothers of Political Prisoners, the Disappeared and the Assassinated "Monsignor Oscar Romero": Founded in 1977 by women seeking information on disappeared relatives, COMADRES works to gain freedom of political prisoners, obtain information on disappeared persons, and to protest government human rights abuses.

compañera/o: Literally, good friend, comrade or companion. Used by activists to address or denote others who are part of, or sympathetic to, the revolutionary movement. Also used to refer to lover or spouse.

CONAMUS *Coordinadora Nacional de la Mujer Salvadoreña*/National Coordinating Committee of Salvadoran Women: Organization founded in 1987 by women's committees from various unions and displaced communities to coordinate organizing of women.

COPPES *Comité de Presos Políticos de El Salvador*/Political Prisoners Committee of El Salvador: Committee formed in 1981 by political prisoners in Mariona Men's Prison and Ilopango Women's Prison to protest conditions inside the prisons, as well as the overall repressive policies of the government. Through COPPES, the political prisoners gained control of a section of each prison, setting up their own health clinics, study groups and workshops.

COPROUMSA *Comité Pro-Unificación de la Mujer Salvadoreña*/Committee for the Unification of Salvadoran Women: Provisional coordinating body established by numerous women's organizations in San Salvador in February 1987, to organize activities for International Women's Day and build greater unity amongst women's groups.

CRIPDES *Comité Cristiano de los Pueblos Desplazados de El Salvador*/Christian Committee of the Displaced of El Salvador: Committee of rural residents forcibly displaced from their homes by actions of the Salvadoran armed forces. Founded in 1984, CRIPDES works to win the right of the displaced to return to their home communities ("places of origin").

directiva: Leadership body (directorate, steering committee, coordinating committee, etc.) of an organization or community.

disappeared: "The disappeared" refers to people who have been kidnapped by government security forces or death squads and whose whereabouts, and very survival, remain unknown to family members, friends or co-workers.

displaced: "The displaced" refers to people who have been forcibly removed from their communities by government military action.

DRU *Dirección Revolucionaria Unificada/*Unified Revolutionary Directorate: Coordinating body established by four of the five revolutionary opposition parties in May 1980. It led to the formation of the Farabundo Martí National Liberation Front (FMLN) seven months later, incorporating all five political-military organizations.

ERP *Ejército Revolucionario Popular/*Popular Revolutionary Army: Revolutionary guerrilla organization founded in 1971. One of the five founding political-military organizations of the FMLN. The ERP's top commander, Joaquín Villalobos, is a prominent spokesperson for the rebel alliance. The ERP has established a strong base of operations and support in eastern El Salvador.

FAL *Fuerzas Armadas de Liberación/*Armed Forces of Liberation: Guerrilla organization founded in 1977 by the Salvadoran Communist Party, and now a part of the armed forces of the FMLN.

FDR *Frente Democrático Revolucionario/*Democratic Revolutionary Front: Federation formed by a broad array of popular organizations, union federations and opposition political parties in April 1980, to coordinate the struggle for a revolutionary democratic government. The FDR's alliance with the FMLN (see below) is the primary opposition force to the Salvadoran government. From 1981 through 1987, the FDR functioned solely outside the country due to repression against its members. As of 1988, members of the front [primarily the Popular Social Christian Movement (MPSC), the National Revolutionary Movement (MNR) and the UDN (see below)] resumed political work within El Salvador.

FECCAS *Federación Cristiana de Campesinos Salvadoreños/*Christian Federation of Salvadoran Peasants: Organization that developed out of the Christian base communities in north-central El Salvador in the early 1970s. Through FECCAS peasants organized to demand land, credit, fair prices, etc. It was one of the constituent organizations of the BPR.

FECMAFAM *Federación de Comités de Madres y Familiares de los Presos Políticos, Desaparecidos y Asesinados*/Federation of Committees of Mothers and Families of Political Prisoners, the Disappeared and Assassinated: Federation of three committees of relatives of human rights abuse victims, including COMADRES, founded in May 1987.

FPL *Fuerzas Populares de Liberación*/Popular Liberation Forces: Revolutionary party and guerrilla organization founded in 1970. Initiated armed struggle against the government in 1972. Instrumental in the formation of the BPR in 1975, and one of the five founding organizations of the FMLN in 1980. Its major base of operation and support has been in and around Chalatenango Province.

FMLN *Frente Farabundo Marti de Liberación Nacional*/Farabundo Martí National Liberation Front: Alliance of the five revolutionary political-military organizations opposed to the Salvadoran government, formed in October 1980. Allied with the FDR in struggle for a democratic revolutionary government.

frente: Literally, front; a broad coalition of organizations.

Guardia: Members of the Salvadoran National Guard, an arm of the Salvadoran armed forces notorious for brutality against the civilian population.

MERS *Movimiento Estudiantil Revolucionario Salvadoreño*/Salvadoran Revolutionary Student Movement: Organization of high school students opposed to the Salvadoran government that functioned in the mid-to-late 1970s, and was affiliated with the BPR.

ORDEN *Organización Democrática Nacionalista*/Nationalist Democratic Organization: A government-sponsored paramilitary network that monitored and repressed efforts by rural communities to organize for better conditions. Now officially banned, ORDEN is widely believed to have been responsible for numerous death squad killings and disappearances in the 1970s and early 1980s.

orejas: Literally, "ears." Popular name for government informants in unions, popular organizations and communities.

poder popular/popular power: Refers to a situation in which people of a community have taken control of their own lives by developing their own political, social and economic institutions. *Poder popular* developed in many areas abandoned by military and political representatives of the central government in the face of FMLN offensives.

repopulation: Organized efforts by large groups of the displaced to return to their communities to live and work on the land.

UDN *Unión Democrática Nacionalista*/Nationalist Democratic Union: Coalition of worker, student and community organizations initiated by the Salvadoran Communist Party in the mid-1970s. Joined with other mass fronts and parties in the formation of the FDR in 1980.

UMS *Unión de Mujeres Salvadoreñas Pro-Liberación "Melida Anaya Montes"*/Union of Salvadoran Women for Liberation "Melida Anaya Montes": Unitary organization of the five revolutionary women's groups associated with the FMLN, founded in April 1987.

UNTS *Unidad Nacional de Trabajadores Salvadoreños*/National Unity of Salvadoran Workers: Broad opposition coalition of union, student groups, peasant organizations, committees of the displaced and unemployed, and women's groups. Founded in February 1986 to protest the government's austerity programs and failure to pursue a political solution to the war.

UTC *Unión de Trabajadores del Campo*/Farmworkers Union: Union of agricultural workers that functioned in the 1970s. UTC worked closely with FECCAS and was a member of the BPR.

zones of (popular) control: Areas in the countryside where the FMLN has displaced the political structures and armed forces of the Salvadoran government. Because the FMLN does not attempt to hold specific areas militarily, these areas are not considered "liberated zones." However, the civilian population is under the protection of the FMLN.

Members of COMADRES confronting soldiers guarding the headquarters of the Salvadoran army high command (February 1988).

Part I

"We Have Found the Strength": Women in the Popular Movement

Introduction

In reading about politics and conflict in Latin America, we often come across terms such as "Marxist-Leninist party" or "leftist guerrilla." These terms give us the impression that conflict in underdeveloped countries is somehow induced by ideologically motivated external forces and that those in opposition to the government are either professional agitators or naive poor people seduced by simplistic ideologies. It is therefore easy to lose sight of the fact that in a country such as El Salvador, plagued by poverty and inequality, political activism for the vast majority of people begins with a desire to change the conditions that oppress them personally and directly. Of course, activists must develop analyses to understand their situation and provide alternatives. However, Salvadorans are risking their lives to change the government not because of abstract political principles, but to obtain a decent life for themselves and their children.

The oppressive conditions underlying the struggle in El Salvador particularly affect Salvadoran women, who bear most of the burden of ensuring the survival of their families. According to a 1978 United Nations study, almost 40 percent of the households in San Salvador's poorest neighborhoods were headed by women. Since that time, a growing number of women have had to assume sole responsibility, as men have fled their homes to escape death squads or forced recruitment into the Salvadoran army. Women's organizations now estimate that 70 percent of all Salvadoran families are headed by women.[1]

In order to support themselves and their families, many women must scratch out a living on the fringes of the economy, peddling goods on the sidewalks and roadsides. They must make ends meet in a situation where the cost of living has soared by 250 percent in the past decade, while wages—for those lucky few who earn regular pay—have risen only 50 percent. A paper presented at a 1988 women's conference claimed that over 2 million Salvadorans (out of a population of 5.2 million) are living in "extreme poverty," meaning that they are unable to satisfy their basic nutritional needs.[2]

And so, in the 1980s, Salvadoran mothers must still watch their children die of gastroenteritis because there is only filthy water to drink, and no medical care for poor people. According to a 1983 study, 57 percent of all children born in El Salvador die before reaching the age of five.[3] Peasant women must still raise children while traveling as migrant farmworkers, seeking work on the big plantations. There they work long hours exposed to poisonous pesticides, and sleep out in the open, all to earn a few cents a day. Refugees and earthquake victims must "house" their families under tents in public parks because generals and politicians have siphoned off aid intended for reconstruction.

The Salvadoran oligarchy and military have prevented the development of any governmental institutions that could effectively address the basic needs arising from these conditions. So the people themselves have developed an astonishingly broad array of grassroots organizations to press for recognition of their basic needs.

It is these organizations that make up what is called the "popular movement" in El Salvador. They include human rights organizations, student groups, unions, peasant associations, displaced people's organizations, committees of slum dwellers, an organization of earthquake victims, associations of indigenous people, a committee of political prisoners and women's committees. Each of these organizations has as a focus specific demands and projects relating to the sector it represents: COMADRES (Committee of Mothers of the Disappeared), a human rights group, demands information on the disappeared and demonstrates against government human rights abuses; ANDES (National Association of Salvadoran Educators), a union, demands decent wages for teachers and greater government investment in education; UNADES (National Association of Earthquake Victims), a community-based group, presses for government assistance with housing, water and other services for those whose homes were destroyed. The Salvadoran government's chronic refusal to address such basic survival needs and rights has led the popular organizations to move beyond advocacy of limited reforms and to unite with each other to press for more radical political and social change.

In the late 1970s popular sector organizations came together to form large coalitions, or fronts, such as the BPR (Popular Revolutionary Bloc) and FAPU (United Front for Popular Action), which openly called for a revolutionary alternative to the military dictatorship. These massive fronts succeeded in mobilizing tens of thousands of Salvadorans who had been previously excluded from political activity, providing them with a new self-confidence in their abilities to effect changes and confront the government. Young people were particularly active; many young women—students, workers, peasants—found an opening to involvement in the political arena, which had been traditionally dominated by men.

However, by late 1981, most forms of popular protest had been brutally and effectively silenced by death squads and government security forces, and most of the activists not captured by the government had to flee for their lives. The only groups that continued to openly oppose government policy were the human rights organizations, such as COMADRES. Composed largely of women, many of whom could not read or write and had never been politically active, these organizations painstakingly documented case after case of governmental human rights abuses. They also helped to channel the grief of those who had lost their loved ones, turning personal tragedy into social action. Many of these courageous women in turn became targets of repression, as the government sought to eliminate this remaining voice of conscience.

While government repression succeeded in temporarily silencing opposition voices, the causes of popular protest were not addressed, and the situation in the country went from bad to worse. The long war was sapping the economy: wages went down, unemployment went up, and people displaced by the war crowded into urban slums. President José Napoleón Duarte, who had been elected on a platform of economic reforms and peace talks with the revolutionary opposition, the FMLN, reneged on both promises and instead introduced a package of economic austerity measures to finance the war in late 1985. This prompted an angry response from a wide range of organizations, including many unions that had previously supported Duarte. As one older woman protested, "Now, not only do we have to live with the war, we have to pay for it."

As popular disillusionment with the Duarte government grew, so did people's willingness to organize openly against it. In 1986, more than 100 unions came together to form the National Unity of Salvadoran Workers (UNTS), which has since expanded to include groups from every other sector of the popular movement. The UNTS is not a labor confederation but an activist coordinating body for activities directed against the government's policies of war, repression and austerity. When telephone company workers were fired from their jobs, the UNTS supported the strike activites organized by ASTTEL (Union of Salvadoran Telephone Workers); when the government failed to provide promised assistance to earthquake victims, the UNTS helped organize direct people-to-people relief services; when the Salvadoran military attacked the repopulated village of San José las Flores, the UNTS organized protests in the capital and solicited international support; when leading members of the FDR (Democratic Revolutionary Front) returned from exile in early 1988, the UNTS organized a forum on prospects for peace in the country.

The government has responded to the successful mobilizations of the UNTS and its constituent groups in traditional fashion, accusing them of being linked to the FMLN, attacking their demonstrations, and arresting and harassing individual activists. Febe Velásquez, a textile worker who is on the Executive Committee of the UNTS, was detained and tortured twice by security forces within two years. Other union leaders and activists have been murdered, prompting fears of a return to the bloody years of 1979-81.

However, the popular movement of 1988 is much stronger than that of 1979, due in part to the greater organizational experience of those involved, as well as to the greater unity between the different sectors. It is also stronger because of the increased participation of women, who are beginning to assume leadership positions in significant numbers. Some of the groups in the movement are predominantly made up of women, such as the teachers union, ANDES, and the committee of the displaced, CRIPDES. In other organizations, women have begun to form committees *(comisiones femininas)* to press for greater attention to women's needs within the organizations and to encourage the participation of more women in the popular movement. These committees have helped to make women the fastest growing sector of the resurgent popular movement.

The people of El Salvador have succeeded in rebuilding a massive and independent popular movement that will play a crucial role in reshaping El Salvador's political landscape. In spite of the government's hostile stance, this movement is incorporating the broadest possible cross-section of the Salvadoran people and is representing their aspirations for peace and justice. The women we hear from in this section have played a significant role in creating and sustaining this tradition of popular organization.

Miriam

"The Day Starts Very Early"

Miriam Galdémez lived and worked in rural El Salvador before fleeing the country. At the time of this interview, in March 1981, she was a representative for the Democratic Revolutionary Front (FDR) in Europe. The interview, conducted in England by Jenny Vaughn and Jan MacIntosh, first appeared in Spare Rib, *No. 106 (London: May 1981) and was later republished in* Women and War: El Salvador, *Women's International Resource Exchange (WIRE), (New York: 1982). The following is an excerpt of the interview.*

For a woman in the countryside the day starts very, very early. Even before the sun has risen she gets up from her rough bundle of a mattress and, trying not to wake her husband or step on her children, she goes outside her little shack and starts grinding up corn into flour for tortillas. Tortillas are the little pancakes that everybody eats for breakfast, lunch and dinner. You really get sick of tortillas, I can tell you! Grinding the corn is hard work, because it's still done by hand; it gives you muscles like a rock.

By the time she's finished, her husband and the children will be up. If the children are old enough, she'll send them off to get water; if not, she has to go herself. Water is one of the biggest problems; only about 30 percent of the people in the countryside have access to safe drinking water, so they're always getting sick. Diseases from bad water are some of the biggest killers in El Salvador.

Once she's got the water, the family eats breakfast of tortillas and coffee. Then, if it's harvest time, everybody goes off to pick crops on the big plantations. Children usually start to work at about ten or eleven

31

years of age, but they often start even earlier. Harvesting means money, and every family needs as much as it can get.

If there's no work on the plantation—and often there isn't because they only need people for a few months of the year—there's still plenty of work for her to do. She looks after the animals, goes down to the river to wash clothes, collects firewood for cooking, tends the family's few crops, cooks the dinner, and weaves cloth or sews clothes. Sometimes she'll go and see friends and chat. If another woman is giving birth, perhaps she'll go and help with the labor.

But sometimes women have to give birth all alone. I remember once when I was still quite young, I was walking along the river bank when I saw a woman who'd just given birth, right then and there! She was cutting the umbilical cord herself. Just as she finished, her other kids came running back. Well, I went home with her and, do you know, she cooked dinner and sent the kids off to play before she lay down!

Sounds incredible, doesn't it? But you see, El Salvador has very few hopitals or doctors, and most of them are in the capital or cost a fortune. A census in 1971 said that there were three doctors and 17 hospital beds for every 10,000 people. You can imagine how many women die in childbirth and how high the infant mortality rate is as a result. Women have an average of six to eight living children, but often twice as many pregnancies.

But that's not all, you know. The women we've been talking about are what we call *minifundistas*. That means they live with their family on a little piece of land called a *minifundio*. These tiny plots are what was left for the peasants after the large landowners took the best land for their plantations.

Of course, many women don't have a *minifundio* to live on, so they lack even the security of a home. They have to make their living as migrant laborers. I think this is the hardest of all; a woman has to migrate with her children from the cotton harvest down near the coast to the coffee harvest up near the volcanoes of the central plateau. It's a terrible life, and it's getting even worse: now there's less and less work as agriculture is becoming more and more mechanized. I think this is one of the reasons why women are becoming more politicized and joining the popular organizations or the guerrillas.

Because there's so little work in the countryside, peasant women have often had to come to the city. But now, even more women are going to the city, because the repression in the countryside has become so horrible. Some find work as maids; but unless they're very lucky, they get exploited both as workers and as women. You see, it's often expected that a maid will sexually service her boss and the sons of the family. If she refuses, she loses her job. The same is true even for many nurses and secretaries, who must give in to their bosses in order to keep their jobs. Women who come to the city also try to find jobs in the free-trade zones that have been set up. They work in the pharmaceutical and textile factories, making things like Maidenform bras. I think that more than two-thirds of the firms in these areas are U.S.-owned. These zones were supposed to help El Salvador develop economically, but the only things that have developed are the firms' profits, since they don't have to pay taxes, and trade unions are not allowed.

Then there are many other women who can't find any sort of regular work—especially if they're illiterate, as many women are here. But they still have to eat, so they have to turn to prostitution and all its evils: the beatings, the illnesses and the endemic syphilis. But what can they do? They can't go back to the countryside, because of the situation there. They're stuck.

The social structure in El Salvador is inhuman. It's important to say this, because even though *machismo* is a real problem, nothing's ever going to change until we have the basic necessities of life: housing, education, health care and economic security. At the moment, most of us are denied these basic necessities, and I don't think we'll ever get them until we change the whole power structure in El Salvador.

The Situation of Women in El Salvador

The following document is a portion of a presentation delivered by the delegation from AMES (Women's Association of El Salvador) at the First Latin American Research Seminar on Women in San José, Costa Rica, in 1981. Another portion of this presentation appears in the following section. While some of the statistics are dated, thus understating the severity of conditions eight years later, the overall depiction is still accurate. The translation was prepared for WIRE and first published by Monthly Review, *(New York: June 1982). Reprinted with permission from* Monthly Review, *Inc. © 1982. Edited by New Americas Press.*

General Conditions

The present social system denies the humanity of working people, using them simply as a means of production to enrich an oligarchy which controls industry, banking, commerce and agricultural production. Life for the workers is made even harder as a result of the political and economic domination exercised by the United States.

No matter how hard our people work, the wealth that they produce is monopolized by the oligarchy and the North American companies. The working class of our country labors under inhuman working conditions; death and accidents are daily occurrences in the factories. Salaries are so low that it is impossible for workers to obtain the minimum daily requirement of protein and calories. Unemployment now surpasses 30 percent, and at least 60 percent of the population is illiterate. General health conditions are deplorable. It requires a virtual odyssey for a peasant child to survive to the age of five...75 percent of Salvadoran children suffer some level of malnutrition. Out of every 1,000 children, sixty die at birth and forty more die within their first year of life. Enteritis

35

and diarrhea, which especially affect children, are major causes of death in the country.

Women have been subjected to a degrading existence in El Salvador. For example, they receive grossly inadequate medical care. There is only one maternity hospital in the capital, and the small number of hospitals in the rest of the country accept few maternity cases. The vast majority of peasant women give birth to their children at home, sometimes without assistance...Salvadoran families are generally large; in rural areas the normal pattern is to have six to nine children. Many women are abandoned by their husbands and must assume the full burden of supporting and caring for their children. Birth control methods are largely unknown in rural areas, but birth control pills are distributed for free in urban health clinics...The government policy of controlling the birth rate follows the dictates of the United States. The aim of this policy is to reduce social conflict by reducing the population, and the program is not generally accepted by the Salvadoran people.

Women as Workers

Salvadoran women face the same socioeconomic problems as the rest of the population. However, they are confronted with situations which doubly exploit and oppress them. In our country, work done by men is valued more highly than equivalent work done by women. Women in factories and on *haciendas* receive 25 percent less pay than men. Children, too, are paid less for their work. Because women and children make up such a large part of the work force, they provide a labor pool that keeps wages low for the entire working class.

In some factories, especially those located in free-trade zones and backed by U.S. capital, there are age requirements for employment: women workers must be eighteen to twenty-five years old. The purpose of this is to increase profits by employing workers who are at the peak of their productivity. Pregnant women are not hired because employers do not want to give them paid maternity leave or replace them during their absence. Before being given a job, a woman is subjected to a medical examination to ensure that she is not pregnant.

In rural areas, conditions are much worse, because peasant women have not obtained even the minimal rights won by the women working in factories. Women can find work in the fields only three to four months out of the year, during the coffee and cotton harvests. There are no labor contracts, no social security, no overtime, and no workers' compensation for on-the-job accidents. Women must take their children with them to the harvest. Older children help with the work, while the younger ones are kept in hammocks in the fields. Children's names don't appear on the payroll, so they are never paid for their work or given the daily meals which are their right...

Domestic workers are generally peasant women who have come to the cities in search of better living conditions. Women who can't find work as domestics or in factories often turn to prostitution in order to survive. Those who do find work as domestics are virtual slaves. They live in their employers' homes and usually work from 6 a.m. to 10 p.m., six days a week. And on their one day off (which is at the whim of their employer), they must finish all of their work before leaving the house. There is no established minimum wage for domestic workers, and salaries range from $30 to $50 a month. They do not receive workers' compensation, retirement, insurance, overtime or any other benefits.

Many women in El Salvador work as street vendors, selling clothing, fruit and vegetables. They are forced to work, either because their husbands don't earn enough to cover the family's basic needs, or because they are the head of the household. A few vendors succeed in renting stands in the market; however, the majority cannot afford to rent stands, and must sell their goods on the streets. These women usually live in shacks in the widespread marginal areas, or shantytowns. Often they have no one to take care of their children and must take them along. The older children help their mothers sell while the younger ones spend the day in cardboard boxes. Street vendors must work outside even in the worst weather. It's illegal to sell outside of the markets; the government says it makes the city unattractive to tourists. In order to escape constant harassment by the police, street vendors are forced to move from place to place. When detained, they are beaten and have to pay a fine to get out of jail. When they need money to purchase the goods they sell, they are often exploited by loan sharks, who lend cash at high interest rates. The small amounts of money these women earn are not enough to feed their families, let alone to purchase clothing, medicine or school supplies. Misery and malnutrition are a permanent way of life for street vendors, one of the most oppressed sectors of our society.

The few women who are privileged enough to study and learn skills work in businesses and government agencies, or become teachers and nurses, jobs overwhelmingly held by women. The salaries they receive are also very low and barely enough to live on.

Many women—both rural and urban—remain housewives because there aren't enough jobs and because they have no one to take care of their children. Housewives work at home all day without pay, and therefore employers do not have to pay their employees for the true cost of housework and childcare. In this way the free labor of women is translated into profits for the employer. Thus the housewife forms a crucial part of the overall system of capitalist exploitation in El Salvador. To keep this system intact it is necessary to keep women marginalized from political life.

Women's Traditional Roles

Salvadoran women are conditioned at home, at school and by the general environment to serve men and to be exploited. In order to keep the home together, women must cook, clean the house, wash and iron the clothes, take care of the children, sexually satisfy their husbands and bear all kinds of humiliation and suffering.

From the time children enter sex-segregated primary schools, boys and girls are treated differently. They develop different mannerisms, habits and characteristics. Educating women to be submissive and conforming, dedicated to the home and dependent on men for decisions has kept them out of the political mainstream. For example, there are even factories, usually North American ones (such as Texas Instruments, ARIS, Maidenform), which employ only women because the owners believe this practice will help prevent union organizing...

Despite the importance placed upon women's traditional role in the family, the reality is that family life in El Salvador has been totally disrupted. Only the upper classes are allowed the luxury of maintaining their families intact. All of the families of working people have been touched in one way or another by government repression. Many women are alone with their children because their husbands have been captured or killed by the Salvadoran army. The majority of refugees, inside and outside of the country, are women and children...

Salvadoran women have suffered for centuries, and their problems have found no solution under the current system of capitalist domination and exploitation. Only a democratic revolutionary government can fully emancipate women—and men—in a new society. Salvadoran women have taken part in all of the political movements in opposition to the oligarchic government throughout this century. Today, Salvadoran women are fighting with our people to win freedom and independence.

A Salvadoran Nurse

"Staying Put, Staying Alive"

The following testimony was given by an unidentified nurse work-
ing in San Salvador. It was first published in Links, *"Three Faces*
of Salvadoran Nursing," National Central America Health Rights
Network (NCAHRN), NY, Vol. 2, Nos. 1 and 2 (New York: 1985).
Translation by Links.

I'm from San Salvador, where I work as an auxiliary nurse. In 1945,
when the government trained auxiliary nurses in all the major cities, I
took a nine-month course in Usulután, in the eastern part of the country.
After I received my diploma, there was a strike by all the nurses in the
country. Not understanding the purpose of the strike, I took a job. I've
continued to work since that time, being employed at the same hospital
since 1951.

Conditions in the hospitals of our country are very bad. The
hospital I work in is typical. There is practically no medication available.
Suppose a man comes in with heart trouble. He's brought to the hospital,
but often there's no bed for him. They admit him and put him on the
floor, or else put someone else on the floor so that he can have a bed.
There is no medicine, so they give a prescription to the family, who have
to go out and search—sometimes in the middle of the night—for a
pharmacy. The family buys the medicine to begin the treatment. Sometimes the patient gets a little better and is released, but he is likely to
return a few days later in even worse condition.

There is only one wheelchair for each floor. If it breaks down there
is no money to repair it. If you send it to be repaired there are no spare
parts. On the floors there are two patients to a bed. The rooms are so full
that even if there were money, there wouldn't be any place to put another

bed. There is hardly any linen or soap or cleaning supplies. The food is horrible. There aren't enough beans, and the rice is never well cleaned. The head of our kitchen has no respect for the patients and doesn't care if their food is dirty.

According to the Ministry of Health, medical services satisfy the needs of 85 percent of the total population. Even if this were true, it wouldn't be enough, and in reality we're attending to a much smaller percentage. We probably reach only 60 percent of the people in the urban areas, where all of the hospitals and doctors are concentrated. Including the rural population, the government probably provides services to only 30-40 percent of the total population.

In 1971 there were 2.4 doctors for every 10,000 people, and 90 percent of the doctors are in the major cities. Many doctors have been killed in recent years, especially those who worked in rural clinics. Most of those clinics are closed now, though the government claims they are still open.

Many nurses have also been killed. Death squads have entered hospitals and killed patients, kidnapping nurses as they leave. The nurses are often raped and tortured, then murdered. I don't know exactly how many nurses have been killed in all, but I know of eleven in particular who were actually murdered in their clinics by death squads.

Until 1977 I didn't pay much attention to these conditions and I basically ignored the political situation that created them. That year, on March 28, there was a massacre in Liberty Park in San Salvador. Colonel Lucero Claramont had just won the election for president of El Salvador, but General Carlos Humberto Romero, the military's candidate, seized power. People occupied the park for eight days. On the eighth day the military moved in and massacred many people, but some managed to escape. ORDEN, a paramilitary organization linked to the death squads, had monitored the crowd, and later they killed or kidnapped many of those who had escaped from the park. My son was one of those who disappeared.

He was a technician who sterilized instruments for surgery, working at the same hospital where I work. He was one of the few who expressed his ideas publicly and he had gone to the demonstration to voice his convictions. My son disappeared as he was leaving work on April 19, 1977. Although he was taken right from the hospital, the hospital administration didn't do a thing about it. The health workers' union, which the government controlled at that time, didn't do anything either.

Two months later, I joined the Committee of Mothers of the Disappeared (COMADRES). I began to travel, to really see my country for the first time. I began to understand that what had happened to my son was not an isolated incident. I saw many similar cases, and many that were even worse.

Nurses in El Salvador are divided about the situation in our country. In the hospital where I work, there are nurses who report anyone who says anything negative about the government. The offending nurse is always fired. Just recently, a nurse was fired, arrested and tortured for eight days. She was released only because her son mounted considerable pressure on the authorities to free her.

Recently, other nurses have taken a stand against these horrible conditions. The Nurses Association of El Salvador has published its demands in the press and sends petitions to the government. Unfortunately, the government in El Salvador largely ignores their pleas. I doubt that things will get better in the hospital until the government changes.

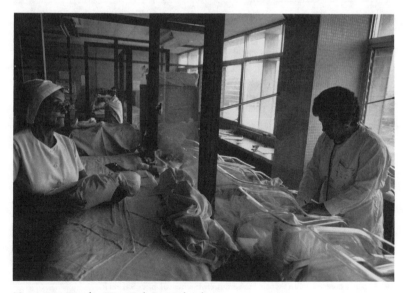

Nursery at Rosales Hospital, San Salvador.

Clothing factory in duty-free zone on outskirts of San Salvador.

Lydia

"A Way to Voice Our Demands"

Lydia is a former union organizer now living in the United States. The following interview was conducted in 1984 in Seattle for New Americas Press by Lipsky. Translated and edited by New Americas Press.

What were the conditions in El Salvador that led you to become politically active?

Working-class people in El Salvador have had to put up with miserable conditions not fit for human beings. When I say working-class, I'm referring to the majority of people in the cities and in the countryside.

Exploitation is greatest in the countryside. The wages paid to farmworkers are very, very low, about $1.50 for twelve hours of work. Employment is seasonal, not year-round. Everyone in the family must work. Peasant women are discriminated against—they do the same work as men but are paid only half as much.

The people who work in the city—in banking, commerce and industry—are also feeling enormous economic pressure. I worked for one of the biggest companies in El Salvador. They told me that I had to maintain a certain appearance and so I was forced to spend most of my salary on clothes. I had to support my family with what was left, but it was never enough. Conditions were bad for those of us who worked in offices, but in the factories they were even worse. Women who work in Salvadoran factories are exploited and humiliated. Factory conditions are unsanitary. There's no ventilation and the washrooms have no running water. Accidents occur frequently and the owners refuse to provide medical coverage.

Those of us who must work outside the home must also take care of our children. Not only do we have to put up with terrible conditions on the job, but even when we combine our wages with those of our husbands, we still can't make it. Faced with this situation, we began to organize to fight for our rights. I worked closely with my union. Unions gave us a way to voice our demands. We came to realize that in El Salvador, a few families are able to live very well because the rest of the people live in misery.

Why did you leave El Salvador?

I left because of my union activity. Like most union workers at that time, we began to pressure the owners for change through strikes, slowdowns and petitions. The owners called on the armed forces to threaten us instead of listening to our needs.

I'll never forget José Guillermo Rivas, a union leader at the INCA factory. The owners repeatedly threatened to kill him if he didn't leave the union, but he stayed at the factory and kept his position as Secretary General of the union. He was shot in the back and killed.

Rivas's death marked the beginning of constant threats against union leaders. We were all put under surveillance. People were taken from their homes and found a few days later, brutally tortured. One worker from my union was taken away and three days later we found him dead. His jaws had been separated and his face was completely disfigured. Another *compañero* was kidnapped on his way home from work. We never heard from him again.

The owners of the company where I worked told me to quit my job. When I went to work, armed men at the door would harass me as I passed them by; they were always watching me. After two of my fellow workers were killed, I decided to leave the company. Although I quit my job, I continued to work with the union.

My former employers weren't satisfied with my resignation and began to persecute me. They blacklisted me, so I couldn't find work anywhere else. Armed men began watching my mother's house, thinking that I lived there. Acually, I was living with my husband and children in another part of town. Well, one day, seven heavily armed men in civilian clothes burst into my mother's house. Their faces were covered. Two of them stayed at the door while the others pushed everyone onto the floor, face down. They told my mother to keep the kids on the floor or they would kill them.

Mistaking one of my sisters for me, they grabbed her by the hair and beat her. When my brother tried to stop them, they hit him with a machine gun and threw him to the floor. My sister was arrested and taken to the National Police station. She told them that she had never belonged to a union, that she didn't know what they were talking about. But they kept questioning her and hitting her, questioning her and hitting her. Finally, thank God, they released her.

They didn't stop looking for me, though. A few months later, as my husband was leaving for work in the morning, men from the National Guard arrived at our house. They tried to take him, but he resisted. He wrestled one of the soldiers to the ground, so the others shot him. They blew off the back of his head, killing him immediately. The rest of the family heard the shots and everyone began to scream. There was a lot of confusion. When the neighbors came out of their houses, the men from the National Guard jumped into their trucks and sped off.

After that I became a fugitive in my own country. For a long time I lived outside the city on a farm with some relatives. In the countryside I saw again how the armed forces tormented people. The army invaded many towns and occupied whole areas for days at a time. They dropped 200- and 500-pound bombs throughout the rural areas. Many families were not able to escape.

The carnage after these invasions was the worst that I'd ever seen. I saw hundreds of mutilated corpses—men, women and children who had been tortured and killed. It was so terrifying that my nerves still have not recovered. So I decided to leave my country to save my life and the lives of my children.

In the years before you left El Salvador, did you see the role of women changing?

The women of El Salvador have welcomed the opportunity to take part in the process of change that's going on in our country. For so long we were kept away from any political activity. But when our husbands and sons began to organize, we realized that changes would benefit the whole family, including women.

In my personal experiences, I noticed that my husband helped out much more around the house after he began organizing. We divided the union work between us, and also the responsibility for the children. After I felt a change in my own life, I wanted all women to share this experience in their own homes.

Women yearn for change and will make great sacrifices for it. I remember how, in 1976 and 1977, women resisted arrest and refused to be taken away by government troops. They were killed in their homes along with their children. Many women stopped taking care of their children to work in the movement. Gradually, we began to see more and more newspaper articles about women who were fighting and dying in armed struggle.

Every movement starts out very small and grows. Women began asking themselves, "Why are our husbands and our relatives being killed? When thousands of people march to ask for a better life, why are they met with gunfire?" Little by little, women have become stronger. Mothers of the Disappeared, elderly women, hold public demonstrations in the plazas. They know they could be killed, but the fear of death doesn't stop them; they are demanding to know what has happened to their sons and their daughters.

Could you tell us about the Christian base communities and your work with them?

I never actually participated in a Christian base community (CBC), but I lived in areas where they were active and I had the chance to see them at work. Members of the CBC's educated us about social problems and showed us why we were forced to live in such miserable conditions. Local priests supported the organizing of unions and federations.

The CBC's also showed us how we could make many immediate improvements in our lives: how we could better our homes, collectivize our work and improve our community. For example, when one family had a problem, the whole community met together to try to solve it. This was all done according to the Bible. The true Word of God and the study of the Bible lifted our spirits. We realized that God didn't want us to live with injustice. We realized that if Jesus were here now, he would be killed along with all the priests and nuns who have been killed. They were murdered because they did one of the worst things you can do in my country—they told the truth about injustice. Many CBC's have experienced terrible repression; their priests have been tortured and killed. One of the main organizers, Father Rutilio Grande, was killed along with two young parishioners. But even in conditions of war, the base communities have survived.

I have heard Salvadoran women refugees in the United States say that it's very difficult to talk about their imprisonment and torture, but it's important for people in the United States to hear the truth. How are these women able to survive emotionally and physically?

I have known and talked with many women who have survived torture and barely escaped death. The first thing the armed forces do when they kidnap a woman is to try to degrade her. She is stripped of all her clothing, paraded in front of the soldiers or policemen, and raped.

During "interrogation," women are beaten and tortured with electric shock. They are raped with foreign objects. I saw a young girl, seventeen years old, who couldn't close her legs; when she was examined by doctors, they found a large piece of wood which had been forced into her body. If a woman is pregnant when she's captured, or if she becomes pregnant as a result of being raped, the constant torture may cause her to abort. The torture is worse than anyone can imagine. What we women can never forgive is that even the children are treated in this brutal way.

One common form of torture is called "the hood" *(la capucha).* A plastic bag is filled with gas, placed over the person's head, and tied around the neck so that no oxygen can enter. As the tortured person gasps for oxygen, she begins to sweat, and the gases eat away at her face. She faints. As soon as she faints, they loosen the bag and let oxygen in until she regains consciousness. Then they tighten the bag again...and this goes on and on.

When a woman survives these experiences, and I know women who have, she is left completely traumatized. Many would commit suicide, except for their religious upbringing. Some women have permanent psychological damage from the experience of torture. Anything that sparks a memory of what they've been through can cause a nervous breakdown. But the majority of women who survive torture feel they have even more reason to keep fighting. I know of one *compañera,* Marta Alicia Rivera, who is touring this country. It's a miracle that she is still alive. She still suffers from the effects of being tortured—she's very, very sick. But she continues to work for the cause of her people. She is an example to us of how women can survive and keep going.

As a Salvadoran woman speaking from personal experience to women in the United States, I want to say that we have been through things you could never imagine. We've seen our children mutilated, our husbands disappeared. We've seen our sisters raped—even little girls as young as six years. All this has been very hard for us, but we keep going, because we want to create a new woman and a new society. We want a new woman to be born from our struggle for a new El Salvador. She will be a free woman, with equal rights in our society, a woman who is no longer a slave in her own home. We believe that women all over the world, including women in the United States, also face oppression and must fight for their liberation. Our hope is that as North American women become more aware of our situation in El Salvador, they will show us the solidarity that we need to win our struggle.

Marta Alicia

Teachers Fighting for the Nation

Marta Alicia Rivera was an activist with the National Association of Salvadoran Educators (ANDES) at the time of her capture by the security forces. After being jailed, raped and tortured for a number of days, she was left for dead in a garbage dump. However, she survived and managed to escape to the United States, where she continues to work on behalf of ANDES. The following selection is based on an interview conducted for New Americas Press in Los Angeles in 1985. Translation and editing by New Americas Press.

We formed ANDES to say "Enough!" to the exploitation and manipulation that Salvadoran teachers had endured for decades. We organized to fight for our rights and for our professional dignity, and to speak to the needs of the nation's education system. Before ANDES, teachers were often forced to work overtime to keep their jobs. They had to work forty years and reach the age of sixty before they qualified for retirement benefits. For the first one or two years of teaching they were assigned to schools in remote areas without electricity or potable water. Unmarried pregnant teachers were forced out of the schools. Many of these conditions still exist today because of the economic injustices in our country. ANDES has been able to put an end to some of these abuses, but teachers are still faced with appalling conditions.

Since the formation of ANDES, teachers' salaries have increased, but they are still very low. Many teachers must work up to three shifts per day because their wages are not enough to support a family and they are often the sole wage earners. A teacher who works three shifts begins her day at 7 a.m. and works until noon, with half an hour for lunch. Then she teaches a second shift from 1 to 3 p.m., with half an hour for dinner, and then a third shift from 6 to 8 or 9 p.m. If she is a primary school

teacher, her monthly income is now 400 *colones* per shift [about U.S. $80].
In the secondary schools this salary is doubled, and universities pay a
little bit better, but teachers' wages still can't keep up with the soaring
costs of basic necessities. In addition, teachers are expected to pay for
such supplies as chalk, paper and desks out of their own pockets. And
it's not unusual for a teacher to have anywhere from fifty to sixty students
in her classroom. For these reasons, teachers are fighting and striking for
higher wages and better conditions.

Our full name, ANDES *"21 de Junio,"* comes from our first demonstration, which took place on June 21, 1965. On that day, 20,000 teachers
and other workers in solidarity with us took to the streets. We surrounded
the Presidential Palace to make our demands known. We were demanding legal status as a union, protesting retirement laws and announcing
our formation to the people of El Salvador. Then, in 1967, we took to the
streets again to celebrate our new legal status and to press for a national
board to hear our grievances.

In 1968, we held a strike that paralyzed the educational system.
Participation by teachers in the strike was almost 100 percent. We
occupied the central offices of the Ministry of Education and demonstrated in front of other government buildings and public places. This
strike and occupation lasted fifty-eight days. The government responded
to the strikers' unity with machine-gun fire; two of our supporters were
killed and many others were wounded. Thousands of us were jailed and
subjected to physical and psychological torture. In July and August of
1971, we held a second strike to demand raises and educational reforms.
Again the government responded with violence.

When ANDES was first organized, teachers joined because of the
union's stand on labor issues, such as pensions and raises. But within a
couple of years, we began to realize that injustice was a reality for
everyone—not just teachers. We began to redefine ourselves, and we
came to understand that ANDES faced two struggles: one for our immediate goals as teachers, and one to achieve peace and self-determination
for our country in the long run. How could we isolate ourselves from
Salvadoran society when we were so much a part of it? And so in
1975—after years of intense ideological struggle—we decided to link up
with other popular struggles. On July 30 we joined the Popular Revolutionary Bloc (BPR), a political coalition of university people, slum
dwellers, market vendors, workers and peasants. At that point, we made
a decision to fight for the national interest.

Systematic repression against teachers began with the emergence
of ANDES and has been carried out by successive governments since
1965. Hundreds of teachers have been killed or have disappeared, and
1,300 schools have been destroyed by government bombings. Due to

constant death threats, more than 8,000 teachers have been forced into exile throughout Central America, Mexico and the United States. But this repression has only made us more determined to continue our union's work: organizing, speaking out and educating others.

The government has also tried to destroy ANDES by slandering us; they say we are communists, controlled by Russia. But if people could see the subhuman conditions in which our students, the children of El Salvador, are forced to live, then they would understand us. Children of five and six must work in the fields alongside their parents in order for the family to survive. We cannot be indifferent to their situation. We are fighting for these children and for ourselves.

The Duarte government presents a facade of democracy to the world, but our union must operate in secret! We can't visit the schools openly as members of ANDES because of the presence of *orejas* [informers]. The government said that since we were part of the BPR, we were doing "communist" work, not union work. Of course, any active union is considered to be communist by the government.

We continue to do our work both inside and outside the zones of popular control. Since 1980 we have pressed for the freedom of teachers who are imprisoned or disappeared and for aid to orphaned children. We've made some improvements in our working conditions, and we've begun to build international ANDES chapters, with representatives in Canada, Mexico and the United States. We have held our congresses clandestinely since 1982, and we have published the proceedings. Within the zones of popular control we teach reading and writing; our goal is to enable our people to learn the truth about our past. Our motto is "Fighting to learn—we fight to win." Teaching literacy in the zones is one of our major projects, and we have opened up twenty-eight schools there with the help of international solidarity efforts. We are also educating peasants to be popular teachers, preparing them to teach literacy so that the children and adults of El Salvador may read and write their own history.

The vast majority of Salvadoran teachers are women, and ANDES membership is about 90 percent female. We didn't find it difficult to organize women in the educational sector, and in fact, we have often helped to organize other groups of women. ANDES assisted in the formation of the Women's Association of El Salvador (AMES). We think of ourselves not only as teachers, but as women, and we analyze our role as women in this society. Part of this role is to organize other women.

Today in our movement we must make an effort to include *all* women in the struggle for independence. We must work together with men to achieve a stable and lasting peace that will benefit our society and allow us to achieve our fundamental rights.

Army roadblock on road to Ahuachapan (May 1986).

Daisi

"Thirty-Two Months in Prison"

Before her imprisonment, Daisi was a university student studying mathematics; she planned to become a school teacher after completing her studies. While attending university, she also worked full-time at the Ministry of Education to help support her eleven brothers and sisters. Daisi's description of her arrest and imprisonment first appeared in El Salvador's Link (monthly newspaper of Casa El Salvador Farabundo Martí) (New York: May 1984).

On September 25, 1980, while shopping in a commercial district of San Salvador, I was arrested by two men in civilian clothes. (Uniforms would have identified the security force to which they belonged.) I was in the bathroom when the two men violently broke through the door. One of them asked what I was doing. I answered that I was combing my hair. The other one said, "This whore has been in here for too long. Maybe she was thinking about putting a bomb here." When some other people began to ask what was happening, the men immediately took me to the General Headquarters of the National Police. After eight days of interrogation and torture I was moved to the Ilopango Women's Prison, where I spent the next thirty-two months. During that entire time, I was never charged with a specific "crime."

Although it's true that one becomes hardened by pain, it's still agonizing for me to talk about my past experiences. But during my ordeal I also understood that mine was not an isolated case. In El Salvador, thousands have suffered as I did. It's time that we call attention to, and change, this situation. That is the reason I want to share my experiences with you.

By February 1981, the number of political prisoners in the women's prison and in the men's penitentiaries of Santa Tecla and Mariona had dramatically increased. In our cell block, many of the newcomers were only thirteen to eighteen years old. On one occasion, the guards brought in two women who had been accused by military judges of subversive activity, but who were clearly mentally retarded.

None of us knew if we would ever be granted a trial. Our families disregarded threats by the security forces in trying to obtain our release, but their efforts were always fruitless. All these things reminded us over and over that we had no control over our fate.

Many women were subjected to extreme physical abuse, and all of us were deprived of the most basic necessities. For example, the quality of the food was very poor; many times the prison officials seemed to "forget" that we needed to eat. At other times they would reduce our already meager rations, forcing us to rely on what our families could bring us. Prisoners also received limited medical assistance. Not only was it difficult to get to see a doctor, but medication had to be paid for by our families. We didn't even have the money to buy toilet paper, soap and sanitary napkins. Our conditions got even worse as repression outside the prison walls increased. We passed many nights fearing that the security forces would come to beat us, rape us or steal what little we had with us.

Because of this situation, we realized that we needed to organize ourselves. So we formed the Political Prisoners' Committee of El Salvador (COPPES) in May of 1981. Our demands were that our basic needs be taken care of, that our living conditions be improved and that we be allowed to have contact with other prisoners.

When the authorities ignored our demands, we decided to go on a hunger strike. We began our fast on August 24, 1981, but we were forced to end it after fifteen days because many of the women became dangerously ill, and we still had not received any response.

We went on a second hunger strike in March of 1982. This time COPPES was protesting conditions inside the women's prison as well as calling attention to the increasing numbers of disappeared people and political prisoners. The prison authorities responded by denying visiting privileges and continuing to abuse us.

At this point, we began to issue international appeals to call attention to our plight. We made a special appeal to women, believing that as mothers, sisters or daughters, they would feel our situation more intensely. In response to our cry of anguish, we received many messages of solidarity, and this gave us hope. Of course, the prison administration was threatened by this support, so they began to withhold our mail. We were also visited from time to time by delegates from the Red Cross, which gave us great moral support and put pressure on the government to improve conditions.

During the early months of 1983, we were visited by several fact-finding groups composed primarily of members of the U.S. Congress and other political figures. Their visits demonstrated to us that the North American people were concerned about our situation, in spite of the policies of their government. These fact-finding tours also informed the world of our situation. The prison authorities were afraid of the repercussions that could come from these delegations, so they decreased the threats and violence against us for a while. We became even more hopeful because these visits led to the release of some of the *compañeras*.

However, outside the prison the security forces started seizing entire families. The men and boys were sent to Mariona Prison; the women and small children were taken to the women's prison. These *compañeras* had no relatives left who could take care of their children, and so the children had to live with their mothers in the prison. One *compañera's* four-year-old son was asked why he did not leave the prison. He answered that he was a prisoner too. When his mother was released, he ran around shouting, "I'm free! I'm free!"

There was a lot of talk about amnesty for political prisoners in February 1983, but we didn't believe it. Then several people were released in May. The first prisoners to be freed were men from the prison at Mariona. Fifteen days later, two of them were killed by the death squads. This was a warning to all political prisoners who were about to be set free. At that point, our hopes turned into fear; the threat of future persecution was so great that we wanted to remain in prison. Some prisoners didn't want to leave even after they were officially released. But by the time most of us finally left, new political prisoners were already filling the jails. The government was only trading old prisoners for new ones.

Once we were out of prison, we hoped that our nightmare would be over. But we were wrong. It was even worse. We had to adapt to a life of constant fear and hiding from the death squads. We couldn't find work. Often we were faced with the murder of someone in our families. My very presence could endanger my entire family. So I had to flee my country, and we left El Salvador to find a life free from persecution.

Editor's Note: In February 1985, with conditions inside the prison deteriorating even further, COPPES sent a delegation to talk to the director of the Ilopango Prison. The director stormed out of the meeting and called in army and security forces to punish the prisoners. Over 100 soldiers and police entered the prison, firing guns and tear gas. Three women prisoners were seriously wounded in the attack. Eventually, however, some of the women's demands were met due to support from outside the prison, including demonstrations by COMADRES at the prison gates.

COMADRES Testimony

"We Won't Be Silenced"

The Committee of Mothers of Political Prisoners, the Disappeared and Assassinated "Monsignor Oscar Romero" (COMADRES) was founded in December 1977 to expose and protest political kidnappings, assassinations and torture, to obtain information on the disappeared, and to improve conditions for political prisoners. It was formed by women whose children and husbands had been abducted and disappeared by security forces or paramilitary death squads. Throughout its existence, COMADRES has held regular vigils and demonstrations to bring attention to government human rights violations and to make sure that the disappeared are not forgotten. Like the Mothers of the Plaza de Mayo in Argentina and the Grupo de Apoyo Mutuo (Mutual Assistance Group) in Guatemala, the women of COMADRES have been a consistent voice of conscience for their nation at times when other protesting voices are being silenced by government repression.

The women of COMADRES are famous for their distinctive dress: black dresses with white scarves, and red and white flowers. A member of the group explained the symbolism behind these colors: "The black dress is because we are in mourning for our relatives. The white scarf signifies that we ask for peace in El Salvador. The white flower is for the innocence of our relatives who are in prison, and the red flower is for the blood of our murdered relatives."

On Mother's Day, May 10, 1987, COMADRES, CODEFAM (Committee of Families for the Liberty of Political Prisoners and the Disappeared) and COMAFAC (Christian Committee of Mothers and Relatives of the Disappeared) came together to form a single human rights federation—the Federation of Committees of Mothers and Families of Political Prisoners, Disappeared and Assassinated

57

(FECMAFAM). This is a unified coordinating body that directs the work of the three groups.

Following are the testimonies of four women from COMADRES. These testimonies were taken by New Americas Press in San Salvador in 1985; editing and translation by New Americas Press.

I

My name is Carmen Campos and I am a member of COMADRES. I am here because so many members of my family have been victims of government violence.

The first time someone in a family is detained by the military forces, both he and his family often believe that he will be released because he is honestly innocent. So the whole family cooperates with the authorities. The prisoner gives his name, his address, his relatives' names, etc. When my brother was abducted, I was the one who went to the National Guard to get information on his whereabouts. I told them where we lived, and I showed them my ID. But instead of releasing my brother, they tortured and raped me and left me for dead in a vacant lot near Apopa.

While I was still in the hospital, they took away another one of my brothers. Then in 1981, they took my daughter. She was a street peddler who sold cosmetics. I went to demand information about her, and a few days after that, I was shot at six times from a passing car. Later, I saw two of the men who had been in that car go into the National Police Headquarters; they were police agents.

In 1982, my youngest brother was killed by the death squads. Another of my brothers was killed in 1983 and his wife kidnapped. Like my daughter, she is still one of the disappeared. And in 1984, my sister and my uncle were kidnapped; they were forced into a car by men in military uniforms.

After all this, I took my mother and father out of Chalatenango, hoping to save their lives. But on October 1, 1984, my father disappeared. His body was found three days later in Santa Isabel Cemetery in Santa Ana. They'd killed him on the first day and dumped his body, so we had to bury him immediately, without a wake.

So this is why I'm in the mothers' committee. You see signs of the government's torture—the mutilations, the bullet holes in my body: these were the government's response when I asked about my disappeared relatives. Thank God I survived the torture, and I have remained here to denounce the actions of these so-called "security forces."

II

Two of my children have been killed, and two others are among the disappeared; to this day I haven't been able to find out anything about them. My granddaughter was also kidnapped. One day, at eleven in the morning, men dressed in civilian clothes took her away. My son-in-law disappeared on his way to work one day, and he hasn't been heard from since.

When I learned that one of my sons was at the National Guard Headquarters, and that the other one was at Police Headquarters, I went to both places three times to ask about them. The officers told me that they weren't holding anyone by those names. They told me that I shouldn't be asking about them, that I shouldn't make demands. It's been four years since then, and I still don't know what's happened to my family.

In our committee we have found the strength to talk about these things, to shout and demonstrate in the streets, to demand that the disappeared be returned. The people who have been killed, we know that they are dead. But our children and our relatives who have disappeared—where are they? That's what we want to know.

Before, I felt alone. My life was spent crying for my children. But my children are no longer suffering and they will never come back to me. Now I'm fighting for my suffering people, and this is the struggle of all the mothers in my country. And so we go out into the streets without fear. If we are killed, well, that's the way we'll die. But we won't be silenced. And we know that one day we will win and the situation will change.

I am a peasant. In all the places where we lived, everything has been destroyed. Our provinces have been bombed, our homes have been burned, our belongings have been stolen and our animals have been killed. The army has trampled over everything. All the people have fled, and the refugee camps are full. The children in the camps are barefoot, naked and malnourished.

We are demanding money for food and medicine. Duarte gets aid from the United States, but we don't see any of it here. It goes to feed the soldiers, to buy ammunition—everything goes to the military. And when government soldiers are killed, Duarte comes and grabs our young people for the army, even if they're still in school. Our young boys—he takes them and throws them away like animals to the slaughter. What does he care? He's well fed, he has his children and his roly-poly wife. We have only disease and hunger. He sleeps peacefully, but we never sleep in peace, because we must always be on guard.

III

Our committee was founded on December 21, 1977. It grew out of the pain and suffering of all the mothers who had searched for their children in the mass graves—mothers who had been to the headquarters of the security forces time and again, and received no answers. We met together and realized that it was impossible to get any information about our families. We decided to go together to see the Archbishop, to Monsignor Romero, to see if he could help us. He told us we must join together and demand with one voice that the security forces give us information about our relatives.

Now there are over 500 mothers in our committee, and we have developed three objectives for our work: we want the government to release all political prisoners, to clarify the whereabouts of the 6,000 disappeared people and to prosecute those responsible for the murders of over 50,000 people since 1980. We have visited government organizations, held hunger strikes at the United Nations and occupied churches. Our aim has always been to obtain information about the disappeared.

In June of 1984 we went to the Presidential Palace to deliver a letter to the government requesting a meeting with President Duarte in five days' time. Then we made our request public and waited for a reply. We came back five days later. After we'd waited for an hour and a half outside, Duarte finally came out and said he was sorry, but he couldn't see us because he was too busy. However, one of his cabinet ministers, Julio Rey Prendes, did agree to meet with us the next day. So we came back again the next day, but Rey Prendes told us that he would only meet with five of us. And he refused to allow any press, cameras or tape recorders into the meeting.

So five mothers from the committee went in to speak with him. It was a very short conversation. Once we were alone, he told us that he knew we were politicians just like he was. We told him that we didn't even know what he meant by "politics"—our goal was to find our relatives. When we asked for a general amnesty for all political prisoners, his response was unbelievable. He said an amnesty would mean pardoning those who had assassinated Archbishop Romero. He was implying that our imprisoned relatives were not being set free because they were responsible for that crime! We told him that the only "crime" our relatives had committed was trying to support their families. We asked him to make a case by case review of those who had disappeared. We knew that many of them were being secretly held inside the headquarters of the security forces, in clandestine prisons or in Mariona and Ilopango Prisons.

Rey Prendes told us that our disappeared relatives were not even being held by the government. He said that some of them were already dead, and that the others had joined the guerrillas or left the country. But we have seen, with our own eyes, our relatives being taken away by the security forces—in broad daylight—and we know that once they've been captured it's impossible for them to leave the country or join the FMLN. Then we asked him to tell us why more than 50,000 people had been murdered. Did they commit crimes? Weren't there courts to judge them? Why were they killed just like that? His answer was that we should just resign ourselves to the fact that these people were dead and stop asking questions about them.

A few days after the meeting, Rey Prendes came out with a statement saying that we had come to ask him to release leftist guerrillas and that, of course, was something he could not do. In response, we published a paid advertisement in the newspapers to tell the truth about our conversation and his answers to our demands. We denounced the way he tried to manipulate us and his refusal to allow the press into our meeting with him. And so we let the public of El Salvador know what really happened.

IV

The seven years of our committee's existence have been an odyssey through innumerable government offices and security installations, seeking the release of our relatives and justice for those who have been murdered. COMADRES is a humanitarian organization and we are unaffiliated with any political movement. Our activities are public acts of denunciation and our work is completely out in the open. We have always invited national and international press to our sit-ins and marches. Although we are internationally recognized as a humanitarian organization and although we are not linked to the FMLN, the government is constantly trying to label us as subversives. Therefore, our work is very difficult and dangerous.

The committee is divided into five commissions. Our Organizing Commission visits mothers of the disappeared all over El Salvador, recording their testimonies and encouraging them to participate in our activities. This commission also gives the mothers food and clothing to help make up for what their children and husbands used to provide.

The Public Relations Commission is in charge of putting together all of the documentation that's sent out to international humanitarian and solidarity organizations. Within El Salvador, we send documentation to human rights groups, to embassies and to the various churches (Evangelical, Lutheran and Catholic).

The Publications and Projects Commission is in charge of producing documents such as statements, written testimonies and the information packets that are given to visiting delegations. This commission also develops projects to be funded by outside institutions, projects designed to aid those affected by the violence.

The Finance Commission is in charge of receiving all aid and contributions and distributing them in an appropriate way. We have very little income, but our expenses—for rent, office supplies, frequent radio and newspaper ads—are heavy. And so we are always in need of funds.

The Commission on Refugees and Displaced Persons is in charge of visiting the refugees under the care of the Church, and helping those who have been displaced by the army's bombing. We have an assistance program to protect refugees' rights and to help them find employment.

As we have persisted in demanding information about the fate of the disappeared, our work has become more dangerous. The mothers in our committee have been threatened by the death squads, who have warned us to stop our street demonstrations and to stop publishing our denunciations in the newspapers. But we haven't let anything hold back our work. Although one of the mothers in our committee was killed and another was kidnapped along with her daughter, our committee continues to grow. The mothers, grandmothers, wives, daughters and granddaughters of COMADRES are determined to learn the truth about our relatives.

On November 20, 1984, four mothers in our committee were invited to Washington, D.C. to receive the Robert F. Kennedy International Human Rights Award. But these women were refused visas by the U.S. Embassy in El Salvador, so they could not enter the United States. They were told, in English, by the U.S. Consul that they were "undesirable," and that they had participated in "subversive acts." When they requested a meeting to have the visa denial translated and clarified, the Consul refused to see them. One of the women who could read the Embassy documents in English found out that they were accused of being Marxist-Leninists and financed by the guerrillas. But this is not true; our committee is neutral. In our organization we have mothers of children taken by the FMLN as well as by the army.

The real reason the visas were denied was to stop the mothers from coming to the United States and telling the truth about the human rights violations in our country. The Reagan administration doesn't want the people of the United States to know that U.S. aid is financing the bombing and slaughter of the people of El Salvador. The U.S. government is afraid that the message of COMADRES will expose Duarte's lies, and so it is afraid of these four women.

Workers, who have occupied the IUSA textile factory to demand recognition of their union, confronting soldiers surrounding the plant (April 1986).

Francesca

"Defending Our Rights Is Not a Crime"

Francesca Romero is an officer of the Union of Salvadoran Social Security Institute Workers (STISSS), and a founding member of COFASTISSS (Women's Commission of STISSS). COFASTISSS was, in turn, one of the founding organizations of the National Coordinating Council of Salvadoran Women (see Part II, "With One Single Voice"). STISSS is a certified union representing all workers employed by the Social Security system. Social Security in El Salvador is not a system for supporting retired persons, as in the United States. The Social Security Institute is a government-affiliated health-care system for both private and government workers, whose employers support the system through contributions. The system is also supported through employees' wage deductions. Campesinos, agricultural workers, self-employed people, and workers in the informal sector are not covered by Social Security and cannot use the Social Security hospitals. These hospitals are considered vastly superior to the public health facilities, such as the Rosales Hospital in San Salvador. The following interview was conducted for New Americas Press in San Salvador in 1987. Translated and edited by New Americas Press.

Tell us about your background and how you came to join the union.

My name is Francesca Romero. Like many other women in my country, I had my first child when I was very young, seventeen years old. I did this for the same reason that so many other women do, because we're so anxious to get a husband, because we think we are getting old and we might not fulfill the role our parents have taught us—to get married and have a family.

I got involved in the trade union movement through my work as a nurse. I started working in 1954, at the Rosales Hospital, where I was trained as a practical nurse. You could start working there as a nurse after only two months of training in giving injections, taking temperatures and so forth.

At first, there was no union at the Rosales Hospital. After working there about five years, I began to hear about a health workers' union which had won a victory that cut our shifts from twelve to eight hours. I was surprised when this happened because I really didn't know anything about the union and I didn't have access to a radio or newspapers or anything like that. But after they got us the eight-hour shift, I saw what unions could accomplish and I began to pay attention. After a few years at Rosales, I went to work at the Social Security Hospital. There was no union there, but in 1975 people began to talk about starting one. Since I was interested, I went to the first union meeting and I joined. We formed our own union, STISSS, and elected a coordinating committee. I've been a member of STISSS since the very beginning, in 1976.

What kind of impact did the union have on your life?

Almost right away there were changes at the hospital. The union got our shifts cut from twelve to eight hours, and more jobs were made available. I was impressed by these improvements, but at the same time I was mainly concerned about my children, my home, making food, doing the laundry and so on. After all, housework alone is more than enough work for a woman with six kids.

In 1980, when the big demonstrations were taking place here in San Salvador, the only thing I noticed was all the people marching in front of the hospital. But soon after the repression against these big demonstrations, the repression against the unions began. At the Social Security Hospital, we really didn't participate in the demonstrations; maybe the union leaders and a few others took part, but most of us were, well, indifferent to what was taking place.

Was there any repression directed against STISSS at that time?

Well, that's what got us thinking, when they began attacking our union members. Four health workers, including two doctors, were disappeared and two were killed. We were outraged that this had happened to members of our union, but people were still very afraid because, you know, in that period, around 1982, it was dangerous just to talk about unions. Even so, our union survived.

Around this time, in 1982, I was asked to run on a ticket for the union's coordinating committee, but our ticket didn't get elected that year. In 1983, we were elected and that's how I started as a union officer.

I was the only woman elected, along with sixteen men. I was working the day of the election, but I left work to go to the union assembly because you had to be present to get elected. My boss didn't even realize I was gone. When I got back to work and told the other women I had been elected, one of them said, "You're very brave; now let's see how many days you stay alive!" That's the way the majority of my co-workers felt, because they knew about the disappearances and they thought the same thing would happen to me. I told them I wasn't doing anything dishonest or illegal, and that defending our rights as workers wasn't a crime. If I was going to be killed, that's the way it would be, but I wasn't doing any harm to anybody.

How did your family feel about your participation in the union?

Well, they were worried, particularly in February 1984 when we went on strike and stayed inside the hospital for twenty days. That was a tough fight because the director was a military officer who had five or six bodyguards and he always treated us badly. It made my family very worried, but I was determined to stick it out.

What are the salaries for nurses at the Social Security Hospital?

According to our wage scale, the Level A ranges from 750 to 1,070 *colonesa* month [approximately U.S.$150 to $215]. The union had to fight to get the nurses' wages raised from a very low pay category. The maximum salary in our hospital for nurses in 1984 had been 650 *colones,* but in both 1984 and 1985 we fought to win raises. It is even worse in other medical clinics, like the Diagnostic Center, where nurses earn only 350 *colones* a month, and get treated very badly by the clinic director. They aren't even allowed to have a union.

Are there many women working at the Social Security Hospital? How well are they integrated into union work?

I would say that about 60 percent of the workers are women. Before 1980, very few male workers—much less women—were union activists, but this has changed a lot, not only because of the situation, but also because of our efforts.

Could you describe those efforts?

In 1985, I became concerned about the participation of women and I wanted to try to get them more interested by organizing a women's committee within the union. The other members of the coordinating committee, the men, accepted my idea. Perhaps they thought that the women wanted to have a little committee to arrange parties, because

before I had organized some dances and get-togethers for all the workers.

So, one by one, the women began to discuss this idea. At first, most
of the women were a little afraid, because this was something new to
them. But eventually twelve of us came together for a first meeting and
we established a women's committee in STISSS on January 10, 1985.
Since then, we have kept on growing and feeling better about ourselves
as women. When I started this work, it was very difficult; I often felt
marginalized, but I kept pushing myself. We had to struggle inside the
union to put forth our projects and to get for money them. But what we
do is very important, working at the base level to attract women and
developing ways for them to participate.

Our committee has a plan of action to achieve our goals of raising
consciousness, mobilizing and educating women workers. To reach
women, we often begin with social events, like parties and dances. Then
we hold "union schools," which are classes for the workers. We've done
this in the eastern part of the country as well as here in the west. Many
of our former students are now union leaders in their areas, so we can
see what women are accomplishing.

The women's committee began to publish a newsletter which
spoke directly to women. The union leaders asked us why we needed
another newsletter when STISSS already had one. We said we wanted a
bulletin that would speak a women's language, a bulletin that we could
control. So we have our own newsletter where we can express our
thoughts, and talk about the union and about women's problems and
how to deal with them. Not just union issues, but also things like how
we were brought up and how to raise our own children.

I can't say that the women's committee has been accepted 100
percent. It's definitely been hard, but as we reach out to workers, things
are developing, little by little, and people are more supportive of us.

Do some women work full-time for the union?

Two of us do, and both of us are also on the women's committee,
so we have to make a double effort to achieve the objectives of both the
union and the committee.

How many women leaders are there in the union?

Two. The Secretary of Finance (that's me), and the Secretary of
Propaganda. There are also two women on the Housing Committee and
two more on the Honor and Justice Committee. All the others are men.

Do women face different obstacles than men in doing this work?

Yes, of course. The obstacles blocking women are the system, *machismo* and all the culturally imposed patterns. We have to work hard to change these things; they have kept us from changing ourselves. But there are really two "enemies": men and women. Often when I ask a woman if she works, she'll say, "No, I stay at home." She doesn't think she works, because her work isn't paid—even though it's probably the hardest work of all! Few men recognize the value of women's work, that it helps them and allows them to work. But there have been changes: earlier you didn't see women participating in marches; now sometimes you see more women than men. This is because of the high level of consciousness that many women have achieved; they've seen that unity and struggle are necessary to accomplish their objectives.

Have the changes in women brought about changes in men?

Yes, the men have changed too. Because they've seen that our role has been important in union work, now they look favorably on the kind of work we want to do. For example, we wanted to hold a party on Friendship Day. Well, in the past, this might not have been approved, but this time the leaders supported the idea. We didn't plan this party just to have a good time, but to bring people together—our workers and people from other unions.

Do men accept their wives participating in union work?

Well, there have been severe problems, even divorces, because of this. Sometimes it bothers a man when his wife is out fighting for a cause, going outside the home more often and spending her days on strike. He's used to being served and taken care of, so he starts to complain and demand the "rights" he's used to. Then the woman starts to protest. She tells him that she has her rights to defend and that she is working for the future of her children.

I remember that women weren't too active in our first strikes. In recent strikes, there has been a lot more participation, but most women still can't do union work at night because their husbands get too jealous. Only single women, like me, can work day and night.

Can you tell us more about the activities of the women's committee?

In 1985 we organized some seminars, courses in first aid and some excursions. We went to Guatemala to visit sister unions there and we were invited to the headquarters of our sister union in Honduras. We have also tried to visit other unions here in El Salvador, but it's difficult since all of us on the committee also have full-time jobs. If we all worked full-time for the union it would be a different story, because there's a lot of interest, but not enough time.

Our future projects are modest, because we have to be realistic. We want to organize social events on a national level and develop the union schools. For March 8, International Women's Day [1987], we are organizing a seminar for 200 women so that the women workers in STISSS can learn about this important day. People in our country don't really know about this holiday and its history, and we would like women here to understand the significance of this day.

Has the women's committee of STISSS developed relations with other unions and helped them to organize their own women's committees?

Yes, one of our major objectives has been to help form women's committees in all the unions. Last year we helped the women in the Pan Lido union form a women's committee and our External Relations Committee continues to give them assistance. This year we plan to strengthen our committees nationwide so that women will stay involved and not get pushed aside in the work.

What is the role of women in the National Unity of Salvadoran Workers (UNTS)?

Women really haven't played a strong role in the UNTS so far. Of course, we would like to see women in important positions, because we've seen in practice that women can contribute ideas and carry out projects that men might not think of. But I don't think it's the UNTS's fault that women don't participate more. It's up to us as women to organize ourselves and to encourage other women to be more active in union activities.[4]

Have you tried to pressure the UNTS to give women a greater role?

No. The problem is that there are few women who participate actively in union work. Most union members are men, so we have a long road to travel before women can participate equally in unions. Women in the countryside are in the same situation: many would like to participate, but they have had so little opportunity to develop themselves. Last year I was at a congress with peasant women, members of cooperatives; I saw that these women really wanted to work, but they never had the opportunity before. We must fight to make the men allow women's equal participation. We don't want to dominate men, but we do want to work on an equal basis. When women are given a chance, we really work hard.

There was a strike at the Social Security Hospital in 1985. Could you tell us what happened?

Earlier that year, the union came out with a platform demanding our rights because there had been many violations of our collective bargaining contract. We wanted to go back into negotiations because we knew that the management would never willingly agree to our justified demands. We went on strike and reopened negotiations. The women's committee was assigned numerous tasks, including preparing food and visiting the outlying clinics. There our task was to talk with the workers about the strike, and help them consolidate their position. As Secretary of Finances, I was in charge of all the expenses. We divided up the work, but the union negotiating committee was all men.

On Sunday, June 2 the hospital was invaded by men dressed in black, their heads covered with hoods. It was a big SWAT-type operation, the first military operation like that inside a hospital. Some of the attackers were brought in by helicopter, while other troops surrounded the hospital on the ground. There were heart patients, women in labor and people recovering from operations in the hospital at the time. Many union members were at a big meeting in the hospital auditorium.

The security forces claimed they were looking for arms, but we know that they wanted to destroy our union movement. Why else would they use this kind of repression? They searched under the hospital beds; they even came into the nursery and searched the babies' cribs! A group of them came in through the emergency entrance, in a taxi, wearing civilian clothes and posing as patients needing care. One of them had his arm in a sling, but he was hiding guns in that sling. They were talking to two nurses in emergency when we first heard gunfire out on the terrace. Then they disconnected the lights, and started breaking out all the windows. The lights came back on quickly because we had a back-up generator. During the confusion, one group of attackers had killed one of the other soldiers who had been posing as a patient. In the emergency room, they tied up all the patients, nurses and orderlies, and made them lie face down on the floor. Then they beat them; one of our *compañeras* had her ribs broken.

The security forces had a list of the people on the union's coordinating committee, and they asked for these people. No one spoke up, until Guillermo Rojas and Jorge Alberto said, "Here we are." No one else gave their names, and these were the only two taken away. Then a colonel arrived. His manner was very conciliatory: he said it wasn't fair for us to be tied up, and he ordered the soldiers to let us go. He said everything was okay, that the hospital director was on his way and that we should just go back to work as if nothing had happened.

We were very frightened, but we knew that we couldn't let things stay the way they were, because they had taken two of our comrades. So the next morning, all the workers decided that we wouldn't go back to work until our *compañeros* were released, the military left the hospital and the director was replaced. The workers from the morning shift didn't come in to work; they marched to the Cathedral instead. When they got there, they told Archbishop Rivera y Damas what was going on at the hospital and he denounced the repression against us in his homily. We also held a press conference before returning to the hospital. Some of us—mostly the women—succeeded in getting through the military cordon that was still around the hospital. The men seemed a little afraid and most of them stayed outside.

We maintained our positions even though the soldiers continued to surround the hospital. All the workers refused to leave the building until our demands were met, especially the release of our two *compañeros,* the Secretary of Coordination and the Secretary General. The rest of us on the coordinating committee put out a call to other workers for solidarity; we received national and international support. A group of women was formed to go to the prison to see the *compañeros.* Five women went and demanded to see the prisoners, to make sure that they were still alive. (You know, in our country, political prisoners are often murdered.) Well, thanks to the courage of these *compañeras,* they were able to get in to see the two men. They also brought the men's wives in. This group went back to visit every day until the men were finally released. And this same group of women brought them out and transported them back in an ambulance.

Women showed great courage during the whole strike; they even went right up to the police and talked to them about the strike. Thanks to the determination of all our *compañeras,* our union leaders were released and our union was strengthened.

So the women were really playing an important role.

Yes, in the STISSS strike of 1986, there were more women than men. The women were out there covering the unprotected positions at the hospital. At one point, the soldiers took down the curtains and the women confronted them and piled chairs against the doors. When soldiers removed the chairs, the women put them back; this went on and on for four hours, until the soldiers backed down and the women won. This time, the union didn't assign women to be in charge of the food; this time, men were sent out to get food. A woman was put in charge of coordinating the strike on a national level. She coordinated the progress of the strike at each peripheral Social Security clinic around the country and she dealt directly with the directors of all these clinics. So we can see that after two years of organizing and participation, we women are feeling much more competent and we are able to handle anything that's asked of us.

Editor's Note: STISSS workers went out on strike again in June 1987. Their demands included wage increases, expansion of health benefits and the reconstruction of hospital facilities damaged in the October 1986 earthquake. The strike was polarized by the Duarte government's refusal to negotiate and its threats to decertify the union completely. Two strike support demonstrations were fired upon by government security forces, resulting in injuries to over 30 people. The military also occupied Social Security hospitals throughout the country in an attempt to break the strike. The union called off the strike in September, after the government agreed to negotiate with the union.

International Women's Day march in San Salvador (March 1989).

Part II

"With One Single Voice":
Women's Organizations of El Salvador

Introduction

The testimonies in the previous section provide evidence of the invaluable contributions women have made to the Salvadoran popular movement. Unions, human rights groups, community organizations and political parties have all benefited, and in some cases survived, because of the tireless efforts of women. Through their participation, many women, in turn, have escaped the traditional limitations of a sexist society, becoming vocal and experienced activists. This development of women's potential, while welcome, has not been viewed as a goal of these organizations. However, it has been a goal advanced by a surprisingly large number of organizations in recent Salvadoran history—organizations of women that focus specifically on women's issues.

The forerunner of such organizations was the Sorority of Salvadoran Women, founded in 1957 under the auspices of the Salvadoran Communist Party. Its goal was to advance women's rights. The group advocated equal pay for equal work, nurseries for working mothers and protection for domestic workers. Paralleling the development of progressive women's organizations in other countries, the real surge in women's organizing in El Salvador began in the 1970s. The Association of Progressive Women of El Salvador (AMPES) was formed in 1975 by the Communist Party and focused its efforts primarily on working women, encouraging them to join trade unions and political organizations. The Women's Association of El Salvador (AMES) was founded by the Popular Forces of Liberation (FPL) in 1978; its initial efforts were directed toward more socially marginalized women such as housewives, market vendors, maids and slum dwellers. Eventually, AMES became the largest, most active and most diverse women's organization in the country. It developed a sophisticated analysis of the role of women in Salvadoran society that continues to provide the theoretical framework for women's organizing in El Salvador today.

Due to their affiliation with the revolutionary parties that formed the FMLN, both AMPES and AMES were forced underground by the brutal repression of 1979-81. They were able to continue functioning openly in FMLN-controlled areas of the countryside, where they concentrated on gaining women's support for the revolutionary process and encouraging their active participation in that process. AMES and AMPES worked to address the very real survival needs of their constituency by developing clinics, educational workshops, literacy classes and childcare networks.

During the early 1980s, new women's organizations were formed by the other three revolutionary parties of the FMLN. They initiated similar types of self-help groups and organizing projects within the FMLN's rural zones of control. In the mid-1980s, these three groups, along with AMES and AMPES, began to discuss ways of coordinating their efforts. In April 1987 the five women's groups announced the formation of a unified organization—the Union of Salvadoran Women for Liberation "Melida Anaya Montes" (UMS). The UMS is now carrying on and expanding the work initiated by the five separate groups.

In the government-controlled cities, women's organizing efforts were revived in the mid-1980s. Women's committees *(comisiones femininas)* began to appear within a wide range of organizations representing workers, students, professionals and even earthquake victims and the unemployed. A number of these committees are now members of larger coordinating bodies, such as the National Coordinating Committee of Salvadoran Women (CONAMUS), founded in 1987. CONAMUS sponsors health care programs, educational forums and other projects to involve women in marginalized communities, and to bring working women into union committees.

Women in the countryside are also beginning to overcome their isolation and coordinate their activities in the countryside. AMS (Salvadoran Women's Association) is an organization of mostly peasant women in the war zones of Morazán, San Miguel, San Vicente and Usulután. Founded in 1987, AMS seeks to counter the devastating effects of the war on women's lives by involving them in community development and education projects. By March 1988, AMS had involved over 4,000 women in 43 rural communities in literacy classes, health education workshops and agricultural self-help projects. It also organized a protest of 1,500 women on International Women's Day in 1988 in the military garrison town of San Miguel.

The Institute for the Investigation, Empowerment and Development of Women (IMU) is yet another type of women's organization established in the late 1980s. Founded by a group of women associated with the Jesuit University of Central America in San Salvador, IMU engages in what it calls "participatory investigation," involving women around the country in analyzing the conditions they face. Based on the results, IMU then helps women to develop projects to address these conditions, and to empower themselves through social action. An example is the Women's Alternative Communications Group, which collects and distributes information about women that was previously unavailable, utilizing a variety of media. As with the other groups mentioned, the primary goal is to integrate Salvadoran women into the public life of the nation, thus enabling them to defend their interests.

Recently there have been efforts to coordinate the wide range of women's organizing activities. The Committee for the Unification of Salvadoran Women (COPROUMSA) was founded as a temporary coordinating body to organize public activities for International Women's Day in 1988. It sponsored a march through San Salvador on March 8, calling for an end to the war and for government action to deal with the pressing needs of women and families. It has continued to function as a coordinating committee for a number of smaller women's groups. The Salvadoran Movement of Women (MSM) is another such coalition that seeks to coordinate the activities of women's groups in the capital and the countryside.

While there is general agreement on the need for a unified women's federation, and the existing groups all agree on basic goals, conditions for such a federation do not yet exist. First of all, women activists believe that their primary responsibility is to strengthen outreach to women at the grassroots level and to incorporate them into collective activities. So there is still a tendency towards a proliferation of groups and projects rather than towards unification. There are also concerns that a unified body would be more vulnerable to government infiltration and repression. And finally, there are genuine differences over methods, tactics and priorities that can only be worked out over time.

In the meanwhile, the many different groups and coordinating committees are working together on concrete activities, such as the *Primer Encuentro de la Mujer* (First Encounter of Women) sponsored by five different groups in September 1988 (COPROUMSA, CONAMUS, AMS, MSM and ORMUSA [Organization of Salvadoran Women for Peace]). Over 500 women from all over the country and from a variety of social sectors attended the conference, participating in day-long workshops on such topics as "Woman as the Head of the Family," "Alternative Solutions to the National Crisis," "Psychological Effects of the War on Children" and "Women in the Struggle for Peace." Popular education techniques, such as role playing and socio-drama skits, were used in the workshops to encourage women who are unaccustomed to speaking in public, to share their experiences with other women by acting them out. Such experiences help women to overcome their isolation and empower them as community leaders and activists.

Given the number of groups and their many activities, it appears that Salvadoran women are among the most organized in the world. Can we say, then, that there is a "women's movement" in El Salvador? The answer depends, of course, on how one defines "women's movement." Women activists in El Salvador have shied away from calling themselves "feminists," which they see as defining a movement of women in more privileged societies to gain equal rights within the existing economic and political structures of that society. They define their primary goal as participation in the struggle to create a better society for all Salvadorans. Women have been involved in this struggle from its inception, and inspiring examples of their leadership are not hard to find. Yet most women have been inhibited from participating by the invisible yet effective barriers erected over centuries of discrimination, internalized by both men and women. The revolutionary and popular movements have apparently understood that there can be no new society built and defended in El Salvador without the broad participation of women and without the development of defined strategies to end women's historical marginalization. Developing and implementing these strategies—which must include measures to address the immediate, pressing needs of women and their families—is the task that groups such as CONAMUS, AMS and UMS are taking on, as AMES and AMPES did before them.

The women's committees that are being formed in unions, peasant communities and elsewhere are vehicles for addressing the conditions of women's lives. These conditions include economic oppression as well as women's subservience to men in the home, in society and within the revolutionary movement itself. Through participation in forums, classes and popular theater presentations, women are becoming less reticent to speak out about issues of deep concern which have long been considered taboo: sexuality, birth control, incest, rape and domestic violence. Women are now publishing their own newsletters, organizing their own conferences and demonstrations—and asking men to do the childcare while they do so. So, yes, a strong and growing movement of women exists in El Salvador. Yet as these women make clear again and again, this movement can only be understood in the context of the Salvadoran revolution as a whole, in which the goal is to create a new woman, a new man and a new El Salvador.

Painting banner for International Women's Day march (March 1989).

Reflections of Salvadoran Women: Participation of Latin American Women in Social and Political Organizations

The following is the first part of a paper presented by a representative of AMES at the First Latin American Research Seminar on Women, in San Jose, Costa Rica, in November 1981. The translation was prepared for WIRE and first published by Monthly Review, *(New York: June 1982). Reprinted with permission from Monthly Review, Inc. © 1982. Excerpted by New Americas Press.*

Traditionally the mode of development of the Latin American economies has been structured around the production of raw materials and oriented towards satisfying the demands of the foreign market and the interests of the bourgeoisie. Concomitant with this has been a high concentration of income, a large foreign debt, inflation and military dictatorship. Permanent economic, political and social crisis is therefore characteristic of the great majority of the countries of the continent; and in its wake, poverty, super-exploitation and repression.

Latin American women, who face a double oppression, have not been exempt from this dramatic reality. Although the principal source of our subjection is capitalism, even before the advent of capitalism, feudal society had assigned a subordinate role to women. The oppression of women is a suffocating cultural heritage, and, as Simone de Beauvoir has pointed out, "One is not born, but rather learns to be, a woman." We Latin American women have undoubtedly been learning: learning *not* to be accomplices to the myth of Cinderella, who waits for Prince Charming to free her from misery and convert her into the happy mother of numerous little princes. We are learning to take to the streets to fight for the elimination of poverty and learning to be active protagonists in the forging of our social destiny.

To be a member of the working class is not the same as being a member of the upper class; to be a North American or European is not the same as being a Chilean or a Salvadoran. We are all to some degree exploited and we all carry the burden of our patriarchal heritage, but unquestionably our class interests transcend those of gender. What has a Domitila, a working-class woman of the Bolivian mines, to do with the wife of Abdul Gutierrez, the bloody colonel of the military junta of El Salvador? For women of low-income sectors, joining the labor force is a survival strategy similar to that of men of the same class and obeying the same necessities. However, for the women of the middle and upper classes, incorporation into production is determined by their level of education, the number and age of their children, and the gap between the family income and their consumer expectations.

There are also differences arising from the degree of development of a region, or from the pattern of urban and rural zones. Our struggle as Latin American women is different from that of women in developed countries. Like us, the latter play a fundamental role as reproducers of labor power and ideology, but our problems arise fundamentally from the economic, political and cultural exploitation of our people. Our struggle is, thus, not only for immediate demands, nor is it an individual struggle, nor one directed against men. We seek the liberation of our countries from imperialism, dictatorship and the local bourgeoisie—although we work simultaneously around the question of the specific condition of women and our oppression within the capitalist and patriarchal system.

While in the developed countries there is a struggle for contraception and abortion, in Latin America we must also fight against forced sterilization and certain birth control projects which some governments have agreed to under pressure from the United States. For us, as women, it is not a question of demanding collective services such as daycare centers or laundries, but rather of demanding general community services such as water, light, housing and health care...

In sum, we are fighting for a thoroughgoing change which will include women in the production process and will free both women and men from exploitation and poverty. At the same time, the search for solutions to the specific problems of women must not be neglected.

Invisible Work

A man's work in a capitalist society is carried out at the cost of a woman's work within the home. Her unpaid labor saves him the extra hours required for the reproduction of his labor power; hence the higher level of masculine skill and the male monopoly of political power. These factors are characteristic of class society, and are due to the enormous amount of invisible labor done by women and appropriated by men through the mechanism of the family as an economic unit.

The family has been the cornerstone of all class societies and has given stability to the system based on private property. The family nucleus is the economic and legal unit through which the dominant classes exploit the labor of the female population. The toil of the male laborer is not sufficient to reproduce his labor power; another phase of production is required, namely, domestic labor. The domestic labor carried out by women produces goods and services: meals, a tidy house, laundered and ironed clothing, and children educated in accordance with the requirements laid down for the new generation of workers.

If formerly the capitalists obtained a given amount of surplus value from the male worker as the principal family wage-earner, the growing incorporation of women into the paid labor force provides them with a further benefit. In addition to the male workers, who are responsible for family subsistence, the women also work (and are paid lower wages), thus making up the deficit of income necessary to survival of the family unit. It is vitally important for the reproduction of class society that we women not exhaust our strength in social production [work outside the home], but rather that we conserve our energy for the private economic nucleus. Because of this contradiction between the two kinds of labor we perform, women are obliged to accept menial jobs which leave us with a reservoir of energy for domestic tasks.

In other words, the fundamental aspect of women's problem—exploitation—is the direct result of capitalist relations of production. However, there exists another dimension—oppression—which is useful to the system, and whose cultural and social roots go back to the dawn of civilization: female subordination to the male and the division of labor along gender lines, which predate capitalist society and are found in most societies throughout history...

In the nineteenth century, socialist thinkers assumed that the cause of women was identical with the cause of the working class. Although these thinkers acknowledged that women's subordination predated capitalism, they thought that the abolition of the social system would simultaneously abolish both workers' exploitation and commercialized human relations. This would free women from economic dependence on men and consequently liberate them from subordination. However, we think that to achieve our total emancipation, such a change is a necessary but not sufficient condition.

It is indispensable that we also transform the ideological super-structures which perpetuate a male/female relationship based on domination and subjection. These superstructures are fundamentally reproduced within the family. The family nucleus is the place where models and values useful to the system are transmitted through the sexual division of labor. The family fulfills this role on a legal level, through inheritance through the male line; on the economic level, as a unit of production and consumption and as a mediator between needs and resources; and on the social plane, by relegating women to the "private" domestic sphere and hampering our social and political participation...

We are conscious of the fact that the alleged separation between the "private" and the "public" is merely a sophism. The private is directly political because patriarchal ideology permeates the individual lives of men and women. It is important to recognize the link between the two areas and understand that although women will not be liberated without a change in society, it is equally true that there can be no genuine social transformation without women's emancipation.

To the extent to which we women are kept isolated and confined to the domestic sphere we will continue to accept our role. We will continue to accept the postulate that, due to biological differences, we are docile and weak beings—inferior to men, but also beautiful and noble—assigned to the important roles of wife and mother.

Changes That Don't Change Anything

There is a growing contingent of women who are challenging the status quo, who are questioning the passive role which distances us from political activity on our continent. There is a growing number of women who question why we must work as much as eighty hours a week on a "double shift" that prevents us from participating in the social decision-making process.

In response, many regimes on the continent have promulgated paternalistic legislation establishing "equality before the law" and provisions against sexual discrimination, as well as measures to assist mothers and children. These are formal measures which do not affect the daily lives of the great majority of people. For example, in the case of education, which is very limited for both women and men of the lower classes, women have even less access than men: of the six out of ten Salvadorans who are illiterate, well over half are women. In the cities, twice as many women as men are illiterate.

In order to avert the threat of a genuine change in the role of women and our active participation in the liberation processes which would follow upon a massive increase of female consciousness, many governments have promoted "modernist" or "developmental" solutions. They point to the betterment of general living conditions in capitalist countries and to the introduction of new technology; they claim that this economic prosperity offers women the possibility of participating in the labor market and, consequently, of having "access to and participation in social life."

These seductive conceptions of women's liberation are almost always associated with conservative or reformist values which are not conducive to effective changes in social relations. These values provide a basis for exalting the role of women within the family, an institution which creates consensus and cultural continuity. This "family" is an outgrowth of the capitalist system—macho, repressive and based on the commercialization of human relations.

We believe that the integration of women into capitalist society, offering them a bigger piece of the pie, does not constitute liberation. No one can be free in a system that destroys everything human in both women and men. Nor can our problems be solved by our "insertion" (the very word implies passivity) into such a system, without our full participation as subject, not object, and without our full awareness of the process of change. To advocate our "insertion" into development, without determining what kind of development, resolves nothing.

First Steps Toward Liberation

The struggle of Latin American women to transcend the domestic sphere takes place on several levels. It begins with middle- and high-income women who, in part, delegate their domestic tasks to other women. Some of these privileged women fulfill their social vocation through works of charity and some are political militants who focus on the structural roots of the system.

The condition of the *mujer del pueblo* (literally, "woman of the people") on our continent during the past decade has been affected in two different ways. In terms of repression, thousands of women have been harassed and tortured, and have been disappeared or murdered by the dictatorships. We have also been affected in our roles as mother, wife or daughter—many of our men are unemployed or the victims of political persecution. We have had to face the sudden destruction of our families and we have had to learn how to survive without our *compañeros* who were often the only wage-earners in the household.

As a result of the economic policies of the dictatorships, women began to organize in *frentes*—organizations of shantytown dwellers, factory workers, housewives, peasants, professionals and other sectors affected by economic, social and political repression. They organized to defend the gains won through long years of struggle. The *frentista* format has become one of the principal responses utilized by Latin American women for putting forward their specific demands. Women's mobilizations in defense of, and in solidarity with, the struggles of men have grown from day-to-day, helping to expose the true nature of military regimes. The defense of women's traditional role, though conceived within a liberal context and subject to penetration by bourgeois ideology, is the precondition for these mobilizations of women: it is not easy for the state to repress those who, as mothers, wives, daughters, confront it in the very roles which constitute a pillar and foundation of domination.

When the private, domestic realm is altered from the outside, Latin American women come out of their homes and take to the streets. During strikes by miners, industrial workers and construction workers, women have pounded at the doors of ministries and parliaments. They have pressured employers for wage increases or jobs for their male family members. They have demanded that the authorities release their men from prison. That is to say, their demands are not their own, but are, rather, familial. Responding to moments of crisis and to the deterioration of living conditions, women participate massively. As the cornerstone of the home, they defend their families; as the ones who give life, they demand that the lives of their children be respected.

Historically, however, both the strength and weakness of such movements have resided in their spontaneity. Arising as support groups for male struggles, many of these groups dissolve when the conflicts that gave rise to them are concluded. When husbands, fathers and sons return to center stage, we women retreat to our homes once again, leaving the sphere of public activity to men... However, many of us now recognize the implications of this dynamic, and this recognition gives us the objective possibility of losing the "fear of power," of transcending our traditional conditions, and of beginning to open up our political space.

The Difficult Task of Being Members of an Organized Movement

If men have, for centuries, devoted themselves to political work and have fulfilled themselves in it, it is because they have always had the support of one or more women who have provided them with children, with affection and with domestic services. All psychological tensions are diverted to these women, thereby freeing men from the small and large problems of domestic life.

We women, on the other hand, do not have such support systems available to us. In order to utilize our intellectual potential, we must organize ourselves in such a way that the private sphere does not interfere with our specific political work. It is indeed a dramatic change when we can organize ourselves physically and psychologically to exercise this role without experiencing guilt vis-à-vis the "neglected" roles of mother and wife which relegate us to the domestic sphere.

For a woman to be active in sociopolitical organizations implies the assumption of a definitive commitment—a commitment which, she feels, will have repercussions on her activities as a woman, wife, mother and, in some cases, as a paid worker. This situation is aggravated by the fact that until now it has not seemed that men have really intended to assume some of the responsibility which has been delegated to women for centuries. It is not easy for men, even with good intentions, to raise their consciousness concerning privileges conveyed by masculinity, to relinquish their roles as the star members of the cast, and to become instead comrades who share daily life and struggle.

Consequently, for those of us who have decided to make a leap onto the stage of history and to become organized political women—protagonists of social transformation—the task as we see it is not an easy one.

The parties and movements of the democratic left have not, in general, dealt with the problems of women with the same consistency with which they have confronted other social problems. Their pronouncements in this regard are limited to the realm of class struggle and thus appear to be detached from political discourse; they do not make reference to the specific condition of women or to our integration in the struggle as a key factor in the liberation of our societies.

This omission implicitly assumes that feminism and socialism are opposed to each other. Women's liberation is not presented in terms of the liberation of the oppressed. The resolution of our struggle is, for the moment, conceived of as technical and private, becoming collective and social only after the exploited sectors have won their liberation, that is to say, in some distant and unpredictable future... A change in the relations of production is advocated, but not in the relations of reproduction: society is to be overturned economically and ideologically, but nothing is said of changes in the family, which is the sphere not only of consumption but also of reproduction of labor power, as well as the strategic locale for the transmission of ideology.

Will the people's organizations be capable of focusing on the specifics of daily life, or will they leave this to the mercy of the dominant ideology? Will they be capable of breaking the female tradition of conservatism and fear, transforming women on a mass scale into organized political activists? The political maturity of these organizations can be measured in part by their analysis and proposals concerning the present role of women...

Women's Association of El Salvador

"Our Work, Our History"

The following article was published by the Women's Association of El Salvador (AMES) in English in pamphlet form in August 1982. It has been excerpted by New Americas Press.

Salvadoran women joining the popular movement have had to overcome cultural traditions and the prejudice of *machismo* as well as their own ingrained submissiveness. They have had to break tradition and win the right to participate in the struggle for national liberation...

Within both the clandestine and the open collectives [of the revolutionary parties] there were revolutionary *compañeros* who, although demonstrating a great commitment and love for the people and for the revolution, also showed a lack of understanding concerning relationships between men and women. Male supremacy continued to be an inherent value in these men, and therefore traditional male/female roles continued to exist and, as always, women were relegated to the "private" domestic sphere. The men, as always, carried out responsibilities of greater weight and importance.

The woman combatant learns to demonstrate her capabilities, not only as a soldier, but as a strategist and a leader. Analysis, discussion and policy planning become less and less masculine prerogatives. Now, every day, Salvadoran women are becoming more aware and more involved in the process of creating new human relations...*Compañeros* and *compañeras* are deciding to seriously and self-critically confront male/female relationships with all their implications.

The Women's Association of El Salvador (AMES) arose through daily struggle against the obstacles that women encountered in their political involvement. There was a need for an organization that would work for the rights of all women, organized or not. Women workers, peasants, housewives, market vendors, students, teachers and professionals all participated in the formation of AMES. Its purpose was not only to be part of the struggle for liberation, but also to gain specific rights for women.

AMES was officially founded on September 3, 1978 in an assembly named in honor of Isaura Gómez, an activist teacher who was murdered (along with her twelve-year-old daughter) by government forces. At this conference we named our first National Directorate. From that moment on, we undertook actions that demonstrated our creativity, such as rescuing the wounded from streets and hospitals to prevent them from being murdered, and braving army troops to provide food during the occupations of factories and government offices.

On March 8, 1980, the first demonstration planned by the San Salvador chapter of AMES had to be cancelled because the military had closed the march route. But we held a rally anyway, and made our demands known: the rights to employment, equal salaries for women workers, lower prices for food and clothing, and an end to forced sterilization. (In El Salvador, hundreds of women have been sterilized during childbirth without their consent or knowledge.)

In its first three years of activity, AMES developed a far-reaching structure. We formed numerous national chapters comprised of women from all social sectors. We also formed international chapters throughout Latin America, North America and Europe to promote international solidarity.

In the cities of El Salvador, we organized neighborhood women's committees, *comités femininos de barrios y colonias,* made up of women from all walks of life. Due to the repressive situation, we must go about our work under strict security precautions. Our *compañeras* provide instruction in baking, sewing, printing and typing to neighborhood women. We visit political prisoners to bring them food, clothing and medicine. We lead demonstrations demanding freedom for women who have been arrested, and we denounce disappearances and assassinations to the Archbishop's judicial commission, the Human Rights Commission and the international press. We work with refugees: teach them basic standards of hygiene, provide education for their children and teach literacy classes. We hold political meetings to provide information about the political, military and economic situation of the country, and most importantly, to study women's problems and raise consciousness about women's issues and the role of women in these times of war.

AMES organizes women to work in health programs along with nurses and medical students. These *brigadas sanitarias*[health brigades] carry out campaigns to improve general sanitation and to research herbal medicines.

Another responsibility taken on by AMES is ensuring the care and placement of orphan children. Thousand of orphans are living in the midst of civil war, traumatized by witnessing the murder of their parents and the destruction of their homes. AMES strives to find homes for these children, to safeguard them from air attacks, and to provide them with food and clothing. We care for them so that they can retain some vestige of childhood and reach adulthood without too many psychological scars.

In rural areas, AMES brings teachers into the schools to teach both children and adults to read and write. The teachers use educational methods designed to transform traditional male/female roles. We also provide political education for women in the zones of control...

In the zones of control, peasant women form collectives and cultivate corn, beans, rice, vegetables and greens. They have also expropriated cattle from large landowners, using them to provide milk for the children and for making cheese. Women preserve food and make candy to provide vital nourishment during invasions and evacuations.

AMES has organized production workshops in sewing, pottery, mat making and rope tackling. Through these workshops we provide women with technical training and a collective structure. The workshops encourage the development of new social relationships between men and women. As a result, both men and women organize childcare within nurseries. This gives women more time to work in production and other community projects.

Women also construct air raid shelters and trenches, evacuate people during invasions and bombardments, and participate in sentry duty to safeguard the community.

Repression against the Salvadoran population has created a massive flight of more than 600,000 people to the major cities of Central America and Mexico. Salvadoran refugees experience insecurity, scarcity of food, jobs and housing, and family instability. And they must face all of this after dark moments at the hands of El Salvador's repressive military and paramilitary forces.

The vast majority of refugees are women and children, and they constitute an important population to be integrated into the organizations that represent their interests. AMES has a program that links refugees with news and developments inside El Salvador, so that they too can actively participate in the process of national liberation.

...The women of El Salvador have taken up arms for the liberation of our country, to construct a new society where the horrible inequities of today will no longer exist. We call on women around the world—particularly the women of the United States—to act in solidarity with us, to feel within your bodies and souls our suffering and anguish. We call on you to stand united with us, and to bring a halt to the massive U.S. military intervention in our country...

AMES meeting in Los Amates, Chalatenango; women are writing to Archbishop Rivera y Damas, protesting his failure to condemn government attacks on their communities.

Malena

"Breaking Down Barriers in Ideas and Practice"

At the time of this interview, in May 1983, Malena Giron was in charge of international relations for the AMES chapter in Managua, Nicaragua. The interview was conducted, translated and edited for New Americas Press by Susan Hansell.

Can you tell us about the struggles of women in El Salvador and the work of AMES there?

Because of a history of ideological domination, we have not realized how marginalized we really are. We have accepted the role that society has imposed upon us and we have not developed our capacities. In other words, we have accepted, without much resistance, that we must work very hard outside the home and do all the work within the home as well. We have seen women as "natural" mothers, as "natural" childcare workers, and we have taught our children to reproduce *machismo*, thereby perpetuating the domestic role that has been assigned to us.

AMES is a large popular movement dedicated to turning all of this around. Now there is a growing awareness in El Salvador that women are a marginalized sector, more oppressed than men. As an organization for women, AMES plans to further develop this consciousness. The Salvadoran movement cannot coexist with *machismo*. We can only survive with *compañerismo*, a consciousness which requires the full integration of men into childrearing and into all family tasks. In practice this is a daily struggle for women in the movement. Men, for the most part, do not participate in childrearing or in domestic work. The

Salvadoran woman can never forget that ultimately she is responsible for the home. Clearly her problems are not confined to the workplace.

Can you explain the relationship between AMES and the other revolutionary organizations in El Salvador?

AMES is considered a mass organization because its aim is to incorporate all Salvadoran women except women of the fascist sectors. AMES works to meet the needs of Salvadoran women within the context of the revolutionary movement. This movement, above all, demands the freedom of the Salvadoran people: freedom to work in peace and to educate ourselves and our children in peace. In other words, we are fighting for our self-determination. But the specific demands of women must have a place within these larger demands. AMES is making contributions that will enrich the platform of our future democratic revolutionary government.

AMES was formed in 1978, when the many other revolutionary organizations were already well developed and politically defined. As activist women, we feared that if we joined one of the larger mass organizations we might be relegated to the kitchen, to the laundry or to childcare. We wanted to work specifically with women, many of whom tend to be less politically advanced because of their marginalization. For these reasons, we've continued to maintain our independence as a women's organization.

The announcement of the formation of an independent women's organization had to be made with a lot of tact. We didn't try to address ourselves to the entire revolutionary process of El Salvador, since this has already been spoken to; we began by defining ourselves as a democratic association of women. Our aim was to break down barriers in ideas and practice, to understand the conditions of our lives. Why are we relegated to the kitchen? Why are we forced to take on all of the childcare, all of the housework? Why? Answering these questions is the first step a woman takes towards analyzing her situation.

Our mission is not to create battalions of women or to enroll women into the guerrilla ranks. This work must be, and is being, taken care of by other organizations. Our mission is to organize the unorganized.

What kind of work does AMES do in El Salvador?

In the capital, as in all of the major cities, political work is very dangerous. Women are organizing in the cities, but they do not dare use their real names. Nor do they use the name of AMES, because AMES is too well known and well established internationally. They work with maids, market vendors and other women workers, but their most important task is to stay alive. This is difficult because AMES is trying to establish a movement within an extremely repressive state.

Our work in the cities is entering a new phase and we must develop new methods. Before the government heightened its repression in 1981, our work was advancing. Much of the mass movement was ready to reach higher levels of commitment and action. At that time, AMES was demonstrating with banners and placards at churches and at government offices. Then came the savage repression in the cities, and since then, this kind of public action has been impossible.

At the height of the repression, 200 corpses were found in the streets every week. Simply participating in a demonstration was enough to bring the *Guardia* to your house. Homes were ransacked, and people were kidnapped, tortured and killed. Most of those who were murdered were leaders or members of the mass organizations. Because of the terror imposed by the state, we must learn to work in new ways. We must be extremely careful.

What are AMES's projects in the zones of control?

Women living in the zones controlled by the FMLN lead completely different lives. In the zones of control there's freedom; there are elections and popular democracy. Life is organized collectively. It is another world.

In these areas AMES is developing new childcare projects. These projects, called common houses, try to address many of the needs women face. Mothers organize themselves into collectives to care for their children. These women also work in food production, and participate in the local governments and in the defense of their villages. The mothers work in houses built to withstand bombings. Inside, they can boil water, make candles, cook food and make all the preparations necessary to survive constant invasions by the Salvadoran military.

In the common houses, children grow up with some structure to their lives, even though the war goes on. We know that each year in the life of a young child is important to his or her development. The care and education the children receive in the common houses help them to adjust to the difficulties of life in the war zones.

AMES's work here in Nicaragua is also important. We try to maintain the combative spirit of the refugees, so that when they return, they will be able to contribute to the revolutionary process. We realize that we are living in a relatively calm situation. We are no longer subject to attacks or constantly facing death. Our work here is to increase political consciousness and to organize as many women as possible to actively support our movement. An isolated woman working in her kitchen or in an office cannot contribute to this process.

I myself am typical of the women in AMES. Before I joined, I was never involved in a political organization. It wasn't that I was insensitive—I was always in contact with the working class. As a militant Christian, I was part of a strong movement, but it is one that doesn't have a formal structure.

As a teenager I worked in the *barrios* and I was familiar with the lives of poor people. Later, when I was in college, I had many friends who were revolutionary leaders. I helped them with their work because my experiences had convinced me that what they were doing was just and necessary. After five years at the university I decided to go to the countryside to teach reading and writing to the rural population. There I met people without even one year of education who had a clearer analysis of the political situation than I did.

I worked with Archbishop Romero in the Archdiocese of San Salvador until 1980, the year he was murdered. Repression against church people became severe and I left El Salvador soon after.

How has the Reagan administration's policy affected the people of El Salvador?

All of us have suffered losses in our lives. We've faced the deaths of our friends, our children, our spouses and our parents. These indiscriminate killings have had the greatest impact on our people. They are the direct result of U.S. aid to the Salvadoran military and are designed to crush our hopes for the future.

Reagan's policies have also led to the destruction of our natural resources and the tools we need in order to work and to produce food. Our villages have been invaded and bombed time and time again. The hillsides have been burned so that people cannot hide from the war. Our farms, cornfields, crops and animals have been destroyed. This devastation is a terrible thing in such a small country that is not rich in natural resources. The suffering it has caused is another direct result of the Reagan administration's aid. But in spite of all this grief and sorrow, the Salvadoran people have made a decision to fight.

A struggle that has grown out of so much pain and sacrifice cannot be reversed. No abstract reasons will make the people turn back. Our struggle must go on because our cause is just and our suffering is real. Our problems cannot be resolved until the Salvadoran economy is in the hands of the people.

Beatriz

"Beautiful Pages of History Are Being Written"

Beatriz is eighteen years old, from San Agustín in the province of Usulután. She is the fourth child of a middle-class family; her mother is a teacher and her father a pharmacist. In her family, tradition reigned—women submitted without question to male behavior and expectations. But Beatriz's own mother rebelled against tradition and decided to face life on her own. When Beatriz was two years old, her mother took her and her twelve-year-old sister to live in San Salvador. There, despite many obstacles, her mother succeeded in obtaining a degree in economics, and this provided an example for Beatriz.

Starting at an early age, Beatriz was forced to confront sexual discrimination. By the time she was eleven, her mother was remarried to a doctor and had two more children. Now in addition to going to school, Beatriz was also responsible for much of the housework and taking care of her brothers. As her political consciousness developed, she became interested in the Revolutionary Student Movement of El Salvador (MERS), a high school students' organization. Because she was a girl, her parents kept her constantly busy with domestic chores, and this prevented her from participating.

When Beatriz finally rebelled against this situation, she knew that she was not alone. An organization to defend the rights of women had been born—AMES, the Women's Association of El Salvador. At the exceptionally young age of fourteen, she was allowed to join AMES. She was accepted into the organization because of her maturity and because she agreed with their principles. She shared their conviction that women could defend their rights and the rights of all the Salvadoran people only when

*organized. At seventeen, she became an AMES organizer within
the Central Front [covering the provinces of Chalatenango,
Cabañas and Cuscatlán] of the FMLN. There AMES had established
a "Women's Front" [incorporating all the women's committees in
a particular area] named in honor of Ana Maria Gómez, a founder
of the organization, who disappeared in 1981. As a principal
organizer in the Central Front, Beatriz has experienced first hand
the growth and development of AMES.*

*Beatriz' testimony first appeared in the AMES Bulletin, No. 1,
August 1983. Translation by AMES; edited by New Americas Press.*

AMES is an independent organization, but like other mass organizations, we're suffering the effects of government repression. The government attacks us because we recognize the FMLN as the legitimate representative of the Salvadoran people. In spite of these repressive conditions, we've seen an important growth in our membership in the cities. The women there are offering their own homes for meetings, and developing new methods of organizing. Now we can no longer hold large street demonstrations and much of our work must be semi-clandestine, but people are still making their demands known to the government.

The important thing about AMES is that we are made up of women from all social sectors, fighting together under one banner. Our perspective is that of the poorest woman in our society and we have made her struggle our own. AMES respects political and religious differences, and in fact there are many women in AMES who also belong to other organizations. Of course, there are women who have made AMES the focus of their struggle.

We carry out work in many different areas. For example, the women vendors in the markets cover their stalls with plastic sheets, which are constantly being stolen. The Treasury Police force the market women to pay a bribe to get their sheets back. If these market women don't sell enough in a day even to buy food, how can they afford to pay the police to get their property back? AMES organizes women around this kind of injustice. We print up flyers, hold small demonstrations, organize support among other groups of women and send letters of protest to the government.

The women's committees often work on projects together with the neighborhood committees. We're working to meet the basic needs of each community. We find the same problems in all the poor neighborhoods—unsanitary living conditions and a lack of electricity and running water. AMES and the neighborhood committees explain to people that we must unite and organize ourselves to gain our freedom. This is the only way we can liberate ourselves from poverty, ignorance and discrimination. AMES's work in these projects fulfills our commitment to promote solidarity, equality and respect for human life. Our projects develop the political consciousness of women and help them to understand their "double oppression."

At the war front, my job is to go from camp to camp to meet with women and explain to them AMES's objectives and how we work. Some of the peasant women I work with really underestimate themselves. They tell me, "The only thing I'm good for is having kids, taking care of them, and cooking for my husband." In cases like these, my job is to get them out of this routine and show them that they *are* capable of more, that they *are* capable of fighting for what they need. The problem is that men, by virtue of being men, have authority over "their" women, and this keeps women down.

But after a year's work, we're seeing that many of these same women no longer view themselves merely as household servants or beasts of burden. AMES is now very well respected in the zones of control, and in these areas active and politically aware women are speeding up the process of social change. Men are learning valuable lessons from this process—now they participate more actively in raising the children and doing the housework.

Recently I had a pleasant surprise while I was visiting one of the camps at the front. I came across one of our comrades, a *campesino*, who was there making tortillas. I felt so happy to see how much improvement he had made. He was one of those men who had been reluctant to let his wife participate in AMES. But when his wife realized that she was being left behind, she decided to fight for the right to take part in our movement. At times, we've had serious problems over this issue. Some men may threaten to leave if their wives become politically active. Then we have to act as marriage counselors, dealing with these conflicts within the group, or sometimes even involving our political leaders.

We women have learned to challenge oppressive cultural traditions and exercise our right to participate in political organizations. We realize that both men and women must be politically and ideologically educated. This is necessary because all women, mothers or daughters, single or married, face very similar problems within the family. And it's not only husbands and fathers who intervene in women's lives, but also their grandfathers, uncles and brothers.

Let me tell you about a few recent actions that were carried out by Salvadoran women that really made the government angry. The first one was an attack on an enemy convoy in Usulután Province. A battalion of women, trained at the "Emma Guadalupe Carpio" military school, completely destroyed this convoy. Government authorities tried to cover it up, but it got a lot of publicity in the papers, and people in the cities were talking about it for days. For the army, being defeated by a women's battalion was a double defeat. For us, it affirmed that a revolution with committed women at its heart will never be defeated.

And at San Vicente Volcano, 150 women of all ages marched down in the valleys and villages, shouting their demands and singing. They were protesting the repressive measures that the government, with the help of the United States, is carrying out in the countryside. They demanded an end to the napalm and phosphorus bombs which have left hundreds of peasant children blind.

The third action was an expropriation of 7,000 chickens from a large poultry farm near the front. A group of women, aided by the militia, managed to take the farm by surprise at dawn. The chickens were sleeping and didn't even realize they were being taken to a new home. Now the people have set up chicken coops and the eggs are used to feed those at the front. Cows, too, have been expropriated. This can be a more difficult proposition, as cattle have to move themselves and sometimes they put up quite a struggle. Food supply is always a priority in wartime and these expropriations are how some communities add to their supplies.

AMES knows that women have a great revolutionary potential within them that has been dormant until now. With our new awakening, beautiful pages of history are being written by all kinds of women: peasants, teachers, market vendors, slum dwellers, factory workers and enlightened intellectuals.

Azucena

"Helping Women to Participate as Equals"

Azucena is a thirty-five-year-old seamstress with four children from ten to fifteen years old. Originally from Juquilisco in the province of Usulután, she was forced by political persecution to move to Aguilares, near San Salvador. She and her husband were persecuted because they had been municipal candidates for the National Opposition Union (UNO). In 1973 she joined the Christian base communities in Aguilares. For four years she worked with Christian education groups and with Father Rutilio Grande, a popular priest who introduced many of the concepts of liberation theology to his rural parish. She taught courses in both religion and political analysis of the Salvadoran situation.

Azucena entered the Lay Ministry after the assassination of Father Rutilio Grande on March 12, 1977. She received her training from Archbishop Romero and the National Commission of Layworkers. Within the Christian base communities, she helped to develop new methods of drawing unorganized peasants into the popular organizations.

In 1979, Azucena was forced to go to San Salvador because of increasing persecution in Aguilares. There she took up clandestine work until she was discovered by government forces and had to seek asylum with her children in Nicaragua. In Nicaragua she joined the work of the popular church there, and when Nicaraguan branches of AMES were founded, Azucena was put in charge of organizing AMES there.

The following interview appeared in part in the AMES International Bulletin, Vol. 2, No. 1, 1983 (translation by Philip True). Additional material was contributed from interviews conducted by Joan Tollifson and Lipsky in Nicaragua in 1984. Edited by New Americas Press.

What led you to become politically involved in El Salvador?

The reality in El Salvador is that the exploitation of the people—their hunger and suffering—is enormous. Through the Gospel reflection groups we discovered that there were alternatives to this suffering, and we began to organize. In these groups, we discussed a verse from the Bible and its relevance to our own lives. These discussions were led by a celebrator of the Word, the person among us most advanced in knowledge of the Gospel.

It's important to say that the Bible has helped me a lot. The Gospel is not dogmatic, it can always be adapted to the times we live in. Just as our knowledge of science has developed, our knowledge of the Gospel has also advanced, helping us to understand our present reality. After the Bishops' Conference in Medellín, Colombia, in 1968, the Catholic Church began to change. And I started to read documents that helped me to analyze the situation in my country. This led me to see things in a new way and to put myself in the service of the people. After they killed Father Rutilio, I felt it was necessary to be better educated politically so that I could fully understand why he had died. I have continued to study in order to learn about the problems of Latin America and the world.

When my husband and I participated in the elections of 1972, we thought they might be a real alternative for the country. But everything that happened was a farce. Once again the oligarchy made fools of the people and unleashed their repression on us. My husband was kidnapped and held for five days. He was tortured because he didn't belong to the official party, and forced to leave the town where we were living. I was so outraged that I swore I'd never again participate in actions that could not lead to a solution. After that, I joined the popular movement.

As a Christian, how do you feel about the armed struggle?

I think that when all peaceful means to demand the rights of a people have been exhausted, and these rights continue to be denied, there is no other alternative but to take up arms. We all realize that war means death, but we would rather die than live forever enslaved and exploited by an unjust system. The people of my country want to live in peace, free from the intervention of foreign powers.

What impact has AMES had on the role of women in El Salvador?

The women living in areas controlled by the Salvadoran government usually don't have a very sophisticated political outlook. When these areas are brought under FMLN control and the women have an opportunity to join AMES, they become more conscious of their problems as women. At first they may feel that they are not of much value; their earlier training tells them that their only role is the traditional one.

AMES's biggest contribution has been helping women to realize that they can participate equally with the men in the work of the revolution. And it is this change in consciousness that allows women to become politically active.

Could you discuss the work of AMES in the zones of control, in the disputed zones and in the areas under government control?

In the zones of control women join AMES quite easily. It's easy to meet, to hold discussions, and to educate people about the issues facing the country as a whole. We think AMES is very well accepted in these zones.

AMES is also doing work in the zones of dispute, those areas being fought over by the FMLN and the military. Of course this work is not carried out so openly, because the *orejas,* the informers, tell the enemy which organizations are active. Nevertheless, women join in the work that needs to be done. When the FMLN is fighting in an area, women participate as much as they are able. They gather food for the combatants, erect barricades, tend to the wounded and organize the people in their communities.

In the zones controlled by the enemy, it is much more difficult. AMES considers its work there to be semi-clandestine. The women cannot work openly. They work in twos, each one contacting only one other person. This is called the "work of ants" because no more than two people can ever meet together. They must always be careful who they work with; a woman with a connection to the enemy could always mean capture. Under these conditions AMES tries any method that works, and when that gets too dangerous, switches to another method. AMES has tried to spread our ideas by participating in the neighborhood self-defense committees that are conducted clandestinely by the popular church.

We continue to work in the face of tremendous oppression in enemy-controlled zones, but our activities are limited. We always work in fear of informers. Already some of our *compañeras* have disappeared. One of our members disappeared when she returned from Europe, and we have to assume that she was killed. I can't tell you much more about our work there because it's so underground, and we know of it only when one of the *compañeras* passes into a zone of control.

Could you discuss how AMES is incorporated into the popular government in the zones of control?

Let's differentiate between AMES and the *poder popular*—the popular government. The popular government is the seed of a new society—a new government whose purpose is to organize the population. In this popular government no organization enters as an organization. This is not to say that many of our members haven't been elected to office. The woman who is now president of the regional popular government in Chalatenango was previously the president of AMES. In order to take office, she had to give up her post in AMES because she needed to have a more neutral position. An elected government official may remain a member of AMES but she cannot hold an AMES post. Officials participate in the popular government as concerned individuals and do not represent the interests of any one organization.

The popular government is the body that organizes matters of health and education, oversees the production of goods and administers the law. The popular government delegates work to the various organizations. AMES participates by working specifically on childcare centers and parent education. AMES tries to incorporate 100 percent of the women into the work of the popular government.

Many women in AMES have joined the armed forces of the FMLN. Does AMES function within the military structure of the FMLN?

No. AMES cannot function within the FMLN's military structure because it is a mass organization. The women who join the military cannot be activists within AMES, but they never stop being members because our organization is for all women.

Have there been any problems with the incorporation of women into the armed forces?

The truth is that it has been a struggle. Many women have joined the popular army, but their being accepted by the men has been a problem. The women who join the army are very bright, progressive and highly motivated and are usually promoted very quickly. Many become squad leaders and then may have to face rejection by an all-male squad. At one time men refused to be under a woman's command, but things changed. The women of the FMLN engaged in a dialogue with these men, and they were supported by men who understood women's issues. Now the women who join the army are more easily accepted by the men.

How has AMES been organized in Nicaragua?

I remember our first AMES meeting in Managua on August 13, 1981. There were twenty-six of us from different parts of Nicaragua, and we addressed the following questions: What role can we play as refugees? How can we contribute to the struggle of our people? How can we encourage all refugee women to participate in AMES? How can we make all Salvadoran women aware of our double oppression, and liberate ourselves in one single voice? How can we raise money for our work in solidarity with the women back in our country?

We left this first meeting with great enthusiasm and a collection of 107 *córdobas* [unit of money in Nicaragua]. We were beginning the exciting task of organizing women refugees into an association that would fight for our interests and those of our people. We formed study groups, and elected local leaders. Soon over 100 *compañeras* joined. As a result of this growth, our collective work and individual responsibility increased.

We held a series of fundraisers: parties, raffles and sales of home-made food and handicrafts to finance the organization. At the same time, we held seminars, debates and film presentations to further our political growth. From the beginning, we sought to share experiences with other Latin American women's groups in Nicaragua, particularly the Chilean organization. We have also shared experiences with AMNLAE (Luisa Amanda Espinosa Nicaraguan Women's Association), and we are very thankful to the Nicaraguan people and to the FSLN for giving us shelter on their soil.

Organizing Salvadoran children here is one of our most important concerns. Refugee children are beginning to recognize their rights and responsibilities. Both parents and children need to be prepared psychologically to deal with the problems created by exile. Through our liberating educational methods, we try to eliminate paternalistic attitudes and prepare children to join the new society. Adolescents are now participating at the same level as adults in our organization. We also encourage communication between the Salvadoran children and other Latin American children.

How can the women of North America contribute to the struggle of women in El Salvador?

North American women can help Salvadoran women by explaining to the public about the repression against women and children that is going on in El Salvador. The U.S. public should know that women and children continue to be massacred. The most vulnerable segments of our society—women, children and old people—are the victims of the total destruction that is taking place in our villages. We want the world to know the truth about what is being done to the people of El Salvador. The army is carrying out chemical warfare and bombings against the civilian population. Government forces massacre defenseless people when they retake a town.

Because U.S. intervention is growing, it is increasingly important that these atrocities be denounced and be made known to the North American public. Military assistance given by the United States and the military exercises in Honduras have as their aim the destruction of the Salvadoran movement. We ask American women to oppose this intervention.

Street rally urging boycott of upcoming presidential elections (March 1989).

Linda

"We Are Going to Play a Significant Role"

Linda Fuentes is the representative in the United States of the Union of Salvadoran Women for Liberation "Melida Anaya Montes" (UMS). This interview was conducted in San Francisco by New Americas Press in May 1988. Translated and edited by New Americas Press.

Could you tell us what the Union of Salvadoran Women is and how it was formed?

Up until last year there had been five different political organizations of women in the FMLN: AMES, AMPES, ASMUSA, AMS-Lil Milagro Ramírez and CUMS. Each one was affiliated with one of the five political parties in the FMLN. Over the last three or four years, there was a process of discussion and political debate among the women in the FMLN about bringing these groups together into a federation of women's groups. A series of discussions focused on the idea of forming a constituent committee that would lead to such a federation. Then, on April 6, 1987, there was a meeting of women from all five groups, and we decided unanimously to form a united umbrella organization that would be the political, patriotic and revolutionary expression of women in the FMLN. It is actually more than a federation, because the five groups do not exist separately anymore. We are all part of the Union. We decided that our level of organization should reflect the process of unity that is taking place within the FMLN as a whole.

So is it right to call UMS the women's organization of the FMLN?

Well, we are directly related to the FMLN, and yes, many of us in UMS are part of the FMLN, but we are not a division, or an organization of the FMLN, at this moment. Just like with AMES, ASMUSA and the other groups before us, women can participate in UMS without being FMLN militants. Any woman who does a task that contributes to the efforts of the FMLN, in however small a way, can be in UMS—that is our goal. Of course, many of us are FMLN militants, but not all of us. And whatever our level of involvement, or whatever tasks we are doing, the main idea of UMS is for us to educate ourselves as women—to deepen our political consciousness and to take seriously the political roles we have assumed. The point is to be able to work and struggle with a clearer vision, of the world and ourselves.

Does a woman have to be organized already to be in UMS?

No, because UMS is also a vehicle to organize women and to bring them into activities that will support the FMLN. You have to remember that the FMLN is not just about shooting and warfare. The FMLN sponsors literacy campaigns, health education, schools for children and adults, many things like that. All these activities are part of the complete platform the FMLN has developed for the people of our country. So these are things that the civilian population is involved in and is benefiting from, but that does not mean these civilians are part of the FMLN.

Of course, we would like to organize more women into the FMLN. But that is a very slow process. The main thing, and the first step, is to reach out to the women of the civilian population, help them to understand their own situation better, and encourage them to work collectively with other *compañeras*. We are trying to raise their level of political awareness, and their confidence in their own abilities.

Could you give an example of the kind of work UMS does with women in the civilian population?

For example, UMS is carrying out a women's health campaign in the countryside to teach women basic preventive health care. The goal is to create a support network that will include medical lab technicians and a mobile gynecological clinic that will enable us to do Pap smear exams—something women in these areas have never had. The clinics will also screen for venereal diseases, anemia, things like that. We are beginning this program by training women to be health promoters in their communities. The idea is that after being trained in various basic aspects of women's health, they can create the mobile clinics in their areas, and teach other women about basic hygiene and health practices. For many women, just learning how their bodies work and how to take care of themselves is the start of an important educational process. So the health campaign works both to educate women and to get them involved in tasks and duties that bring them together.

You have to keep in mind that this is a long process. We can't just say, "This is what we'll do," and immediately implement it. The health campaigns, for example, start out in settlements near FMLN encampments, and then eventually involve more people and move into other communities. Maybe when we start in a village, some of the people will not want to participate. But they observe how it works, and the next time they want to get involved, too. We see this as an educational process, a first step in developing women's consciousness about their role in the revolutionary process.

Of course, women have been involved in the struggle all along. But most of the time, we were two steps behind the *compañeros* [i.e., the men]. That is why we must develop our political and social awareness, so we can discuss our situation as women, and participate fully in the decisions about our country's future. That is the goal of UMS.

How does UMS overcome the obstacles to greater participation by women?

Well, one thing we do is get together to discuss our right to participate fully in the struggle. We are moving away from a time when we were passive objects, and instead are learning to see ourselves as capable agents of social change. That is the idea, that we give more relevance to our own experiences as women.

And we don't just discuss this among ourselves. We also talk with the *compañeros,* because frankly, there has been a certain closed-mindedness on their part. There are men who are very involved in the struggle, and who work very hard, but who haven't bothered to encourage their own *compañeras* politically. So we try to talk to them about educating their wives and allowing them time to go to meetings or study groups. We encourage the men to take on some of the housework, so that their *compañeras* can also have a chance to develop themselves as human beings, as capable women, and to become more involved politically.

So we are making an effort to generate discussion and political debate about these issues, to get the *compañeras* and *compañeros* together to listen to each other and to talk about how we feel. Of course, some of the *compañeros,* whose political consciousness isn't very developed, say things like, "There they go, doing their 'feminist' work." So you see, there is still a lot of prejudice.

Do you think what's happening now in El Salvador in terms of the women's movement is a kind of feminism? Our understanding is that that term is not very well received.

Yes, that has been true. We've been pretty ignorant about feminism; as a woman I recognize that. I used to think feminism was for upper- and middle-class women who had nothing better to do than sit around and discuss things that, for the most part, were irrelevant to women in the rest of the world, who live under terrible oppression. It even occurred to me that feminism might be an imperialist maneuver to divide society and get women wrapped up in something that would divert them from the real problem, which is the whole system of oppression. Of course, this oppression is more subtle in the United States than in El Salvador, but even if you don't see it, it still exists, and affects both men and women.

But when I came to the United States I began to realize that there are different kinds of feminism. I can relate to some of them because they aren't divisive, but have a progressive perspective, advocating human liberation. So for me now, feminism has become an expression of women who take themselves seriously as people and as human beings capable of development.

Do women experience a different level of oppression than men in El Salvador?

Yes, we can say that their oppression is definitely worse. For example, about 80 percent of Salvadoran women are illiterate, which is much higher than the overall rate. This is because most women don't have access to an education. In the countryside, parents prefer to send their sons to school, rather than their daughters. So women have a harder time finding jobs, and their rate of unemployment and underemployment is higher than for men. These are real, concrete forms of oppression for women.

Has UMS found any contradiction between trying to meet women's very serious current needs and organizing to bring more women into the revolutionary struggle?

There's no contradiction, because we're laying the foundation for the future. As we develop our consciousness as women, our participation in the revolution becomes much more meaningful. Otherwise, we put off the process, we put off education and women's development until some time in the future. And we don't want that to happen. We've been put off for too long. Now the revolutionary process itself is giving us the opportunity to discover how important it is for us to wake up! This is the moment to direct ourselves toward the future as women. We are going to play a significant part in this revolution.

Of course, women have been playing an important role all along, that's important to recognize. In the human rights movement, organizations such as FECMAFAM are made up almost entirely of women. And in the FMLN itself, 30 percent of the leadership is made up of women, and the rank and file is about 40 percent women. But our demand is to go even further, as women. UMS is a product of this aspiration. We've arrived at a point where our demands, politically speaking, are greater than they were before. And our effort at this time must be to get from here...to there, as women.

Do you think the revolution could succeed without women achieving the level of involvement you are striving for?

Well, to a degree, yes. But it would be at a disadvantage. Because to the extent that we are integrated as Salvadorans, all together, we will have a greater capacity to consolidate our revolution and ensure our triumph. The degree of our participation will not change the ideals and political ideology behind the revolution, but it will make them stronger and more consistent.

Why is that?

Because the revolutionary process is about developing human beings, regardless of sex. To the degree that we develop ourselves ideologically and politically, any social transformation will be stronger and harder to defeat. But the reason we have to talk about ourselves "as women" is because we have been historically relegated to less significant tasks in society, and because we have not had the opportunities to develop our capacities. With the situation in our country approaching a decisive stage, circumstances demand the highest possible participation from everyone. We women have participated less in the past, and now is the moment for us to change that. And so UMS appears at this juncture, to encourage and consolidate the involvement of women at this critical time.

So how does UMS bring in these new women who have not yet been organized?

Well, mostly UMS offers a woman the opportunity to join an organized effort, to educate herself and to work with other *compañeras*. We can't make the choice for her—each woman has to take that first step by herself. But we can provide mechanisms, like the health campaign, that open up opportunities. You see, we can't just come into a community and call all the women together to sit down and talk things over. You have to remember the context of living in the midst of a war. Discussions will take place while we're treating someone who is sick or wounded, or while we're watching over the children. That's how things have to happen—simultaneously. We don't have schedules like you do here, where you know you're going to have a meeting at a particular time, in a particular place. No, we can't afford to program things like that. Today, we are here, we can talk. Tomorrow we don't know where we'll be. It's important to have that flexibility. And, practically speaking, in the midst of the war, that's how the *compañeras* and *compañeros* operate.

One more question. What is the relationship of UMS to the new women's coalitions in the government-controlled areas, such as CONAMUS and COPROUMSA?

We don't have a formal relationship. We both arise from the historical necessity to strengthen the movement for a new El Salvador by integrating women in a meaningful way. But we operate on different levels. UMS works at a higher political level, within the FMLN. COPROUMSA functions at the level of the mass movement, with a concrete platform of demands, including an end to U.S. intervention in El Salvador, respect for human rights, better wages and working conditions, etc. COPROUMSA is made up of women's groups from all sectors of the mass movement, including the UNTS, CRIPDES and FECMAFAM. Its goal is to stimulate the consolidation of women within the popular movement. With the creation of a broad coalition representing their demands, women are participating more fully, and more militantly, in the mass movement.

So UMS and COPROUMSA are related organizations in that we have the same goals, for women and for El Salvador. But we are not part of the same entity and we do not work together. The enemy will try to make connections, to accuse COPROUMSA of being UMS and part of the FMLN. But we are not the same, even though we're doing similar things, and we cannot allow the government to use this to attack the mass movement. So the distinction is important. We spring from the same well, but we are not in the same bucket. At the same time, we understand that the struggles of the FMLN and the mass movement couldn't exist without each other.

So the relationship between UMS and COPROUMSA is that we respond to the same specific conditions. These conditions have created two instruments, or vehicles, for the optimum organization for the women of El Salvador, so that we can achieve the level of combative participation that is so necessary at this point in our struggle. That new sectors of women are advancing to join in the work shows that the process is not stuck, that the train of history is moving forward and will not pass us by.

CONAMUS

The People's School: A Woman's Body

The National Coordinating Committee of Salvadoran Women (CONAMUS) was founded in early 1987 by women's committees from seventeen different unions and student associations, joined by women from the cooperative movement and independent professionals and housewives. It is a public organization that functions in government-controlled areas of El Salvador to organize and consolidate women in support of a spectrum of popular demands. Along with its various activities (forums, demonstrations, publications), CONAMUS is participating in discussions with other women's committees about the formation of a unitary women's federation. Its basic organizational goals are explained in an editorial appearing in the first issue of the CONAMUS Bulletin, Voz y Acción de la Mujer (Women's Voice and Action), Summer 1987 (translated and edited by New Americas Press):

"El Salvador...is a country with a long history of dictatorships, exploitation and poverty, yet where the popular classes are making rapid headway in their search for decent and fair living conditions...[and] for peace, which is the highest aspiration of the Salvadoran people.

"The National Coordinating Committee of Salvadoran Women (CONAMUS) has emerged within this framework, encompassing organizations from different social sectors (peasants, workers, students, cooperative members, etc.). Our basic objectives are: 1. To raise the consciousness of women so that we can understand our situation and participate in changing it. 2. To coordinate the various efforts to advance women, in order to unify and empower ourselves on a national level.

"...Both CONAMUS and the Bulletin are conceived in the spirit of solidarity and unity. We are not a sexist or divisive

113

organization, but are fundamentally dedicated to the advance-ment of the majority classes of our country, as well as to the strengthening and development of women for our own growth... We do not want a battle between the sexes, but rather the integration and strengthening of men and women together so that we can achieve a more just and democratic society."

The Bulletin, *directed to a wide range of activist and unor-ganized women, contains poetry, recipes, cartoons, news briefs and educational articles. The following article on women's sexu-ality appeared in the Summer 1987 issue of the* Bulletin; *it has been translated by New Americas Press.*

Human sexuality is a natural and necessary part of our lives. Whether we are men or women, sexuality is an expression of our need to communicate with, and be close to, other people. Our sexuality is tied in with how we think about our own bodies and those of other people, with our feelings, thoughts and actions.

Sexuality can be expressed in many ways: through feelings and affection, and through our bodies. It doesn't matter how old we are—whether we are young or old, divorced, widowed or single, mentally or physically handicapped—all of us have natural sexual needs and desires.

Our sexuality is expressed in our desire to speak with and to understand one another, to laugh together, to exchange glances, to caress one another; all of these make the union of our bodies a pro-foundly human experience. Our bodies are capable of experiencing deep pleasure when there is open communication between people. However, most of us don't experience sexuality in this way.

We have been taught that our sexuality has to do only with genital relations, and that it's something private, secret and even shameful. We don't think of our sexuality as something that is connected with social relations, history, our work or the economic system.

The result is that our experience of our sexuality is limited and repressed. Because it is considered private and we rarely talk about it, we assume that the way we experience sexuality is something we can't question, something that has to be this way because that's how we are created. We have been led to believe that there are certain characteristics, or ways of being, that automatically correspond to each sex. We believe, for example, that masculinity is what makes men aggressive, uncontrol-lable, decisive, strong, active and the possessors of women. And we believe that femininity makes women passive, patient, obedient, weak, dependent on men, fulfilled only when we have children, and always ready to please and meet the needs of others, without thinking of our own needs.

However, men and women don't have to be this way. These characteristics are not inherited and do not depend on one's sex or on one's sexual organs. From the time we were small children we were taught to behave this way by our families and society. Society forces women to limit our sexuality so that it only serves to produce children and to satisfy our husbands' needs.

In our capitalist society it is essential that the family continue to function the way it always has and that women continue to fulfill their traditional roles. We are threatened with damnation if we decide to change because:

—Women reproduce (give birth, raise and educate the children) within the family. Our children are the future workers needed by society.

—In order to control the reproduction of workers, society pressures women to marry and not to have children outside of marriage.

—Society also controls the number of children women have by prohibiting birth control when a higher birthrate is desired, and by imposing birth control measures when they think there are too many of us.

—Prohibiting abortion is another way of taking away women's control over our own bodies and our right to decide whether or not to have children.

—Women's ignorance about our bodies undermines our sense of self-worth and enables men to use us for their own needs.

—Within the family, women function to restore the energy of the working class. If we did not take care of the workers, they would not be able to produce as much.

If all these services were not provided for free, the bosses would lose out!

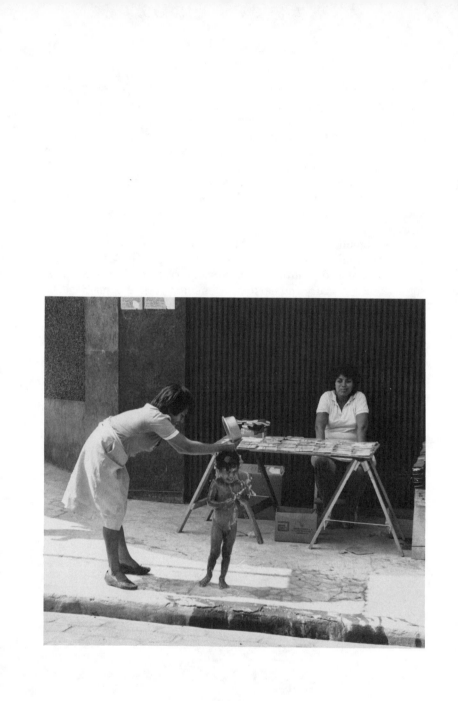

Women and the Family in El Salvador

The following presentation was delivered by Carmen Virginia Martinez at the International Women's Day Forum sponsored by CONAMUS on March 6, 1988. Translated and edited by New Americas Press.

Introduction

On previous occasions we have discussed the legal structure under which women must live—a structure rendered by tradition into a civil code that conceives of women as dependent, submissive and passive beings, and thus reveals the basic sexist design of this society. The supposed constitutional equality of men and women has been shown to be an empty theoretical construct that is inoperative in the functioning of our legal institutions.

We have also discussed how the majority of women are employed in service or secondary, marginal activities that do not produce capital, so that consequently they have little clout as a labor force. We have also dealt with women's role in domestic labor—labor which provides for the reproduction and sustenance of the workforce but which is given no economic value. And in terms of health conditions, education and other general social services for women and children, we know from our own experience how terribly deficient and inadequate these are.

At the present time, we will focus on the issue of women as social beings of the female sex. We will discuss the forces which affect a woman as part of a couple, and motherhood as one of her functions within that unit.

Woman as Part of a Couple

We may begin by acknowledging that the couple is a unit formed on the basis of a love relationship. However, this sentiment of love as a cultural expression is regulated by the predominant values of a society which, because of its socio-economic nature, conditions its members to reproduce sexist cultural values. The concept of Love, therefore, is interpreted in light of these values.

"Love" has been well utilized as a fundamental mechanism in the manipulation and oppression of women. This emotion, however, remains an existential necessity for all human beings. Erich Fromm interprets love as the power to overcome barriers, to unite us with others and to overcome isolation. According to Fromm, it is love which allows us, ultimately, to be fully ourselves and to maintain our personal integrity.

This vision of love as a positive force for self-realization is corrupted and distorted by a world of unequal social relations... In such a society, women enter life at a disadvantage. Subordinated to men and economically dependent, they find themselves in a situation fraught with difficulties and limitations as they search for self-realization and the fulfillment of their need for love. Although a woman participates in the selection of her partner, she must do so in a passive way. Her loved one must be someone who has the means to support her. Therefore, her selection cannot be spontaneous. She must make sure that the man she chooses can give her not only emotional security, but also economic security.

Once a part of a couple, a woman must maintain this union even though she may realize that her situation leaves her unsatisfied, empty and bored. Even in her intimate sexual relations, she is stripped of her dignity and thus loses part of her value as a human being. This kind of subjugation is so generalized in our society that it is considered normal and natural. Thus, in El Salvador, a great percentage of women are thwarted in their efforts to be authentic human beings.

Often, these untenable situations lead to sick relationships in which a woman is subjected to violence and threatened with even worse treatment if she talks about what is happening to her. The truth is not revealed until the woman, her mental and physical health destroyed, seeks medical attention, and even then she may insist on covering up the situation.

Through my own work, I have seen women whose husbands have scalded their vaginas, and others who have had to be hospitalized for up to a month or more to recover from a husband's beating. I have seen women who have been under psychiatric care for ten or fifteen years and who still refuse to separate from their husbands until their children are grown. Profound scars remain in the home and they are difficult to erase. These women are afraid to denounce their husbands because it is the men who support the families and separation would mean seeking help from parents or siblings. In cases where abused wives seek legal protection, they find no assistance. What difference does it make to cite numerous articles or chapters of a legal code if in practice the judicial apparatus and its personnel are cut from the same sexist cloth? These situations occur because the partners women are forced to choose are themselves products of the *machismo* and violence of a society in complete social crisis. No matter how strong or determined a woman may be, she must still withstand humiliation and sexual degradation.

On the other hand, we also see the disintegration of traditional family ties. The formation of conjugal bonds is at a low point. The marriage rate in 1974 was only 4.24 per 1,000 inhabitants, compared to the 10 per 1,000 that was considered normal. In rural areas we see a marked reduction in this rate from 2.48 per 1,000 in 1976 to 1.98 per 1,000 in 1982.

This disintegration of the couple and the traditional family can be explained by a number of factors. Our culture encourages sexist conduct and tolerates the masculine irresponsibility which leaves women solely responsible for their children's upbringing and education. Conditions are aggravated by the wartime crisis in our country, which has forced many men to emigrate abroad to support their families. In many cases, the women lose contact with these men (and thus with their only means of support). And often, men who wish to return to El Salvador cannot do so because of the unemployment, hunger and repression.

Other women are left alone to care for their families when their men are forcibly recruited into the Salvadoran army... In other cases, men get fed up with the injustice and poverty, and leave to join the guerrillas. Many women become heads of households when their partners are kidnapped or suddenly disappear, and none of the military branches or human rights groups can offer information on their whereabouts. Due to such conditions, a high percentage of Salvadoran families have been reduced to a single mother and her children.

What, we may ask, will become of the fabric of Salvadoran society if the family—the fundamental institution that provides for the reproduction and nurturing of the individual, that satisfies our needs and transmits our cultural values—is being openly and profoundly altered?

Woman in her Role as Mother

We will not discuss in detail the philosophical underpinnings of maternity. Let us begin, instead, with an undeniable reality in El Salvador: Our women are deprived of the most essential means of carrying out the important function of motherhood.

Although the constitution formally acknowledges society's obligation to the family, in practice this is nowhere in evidence. The government's provisions for the protection of mothers are scarce or inoperative. There is only one maternity hospital in the whole country. We can easily see the lack of adequate resources to assure the health of our children. Malnutrition and intestinal parasites are a daily reality in our society. The constitution also states that there should be childcare facilities near industrial centers, to serve the needs of working mothers. But what does this legality mean if working women find it impossible to demand services? And peasant women in the rural areas must carry out their maternal role under conditions that are even more primitive and miserable. Women are gravely affected by the wartime crisis. Unemployment is so high that mothers are forced to work in the marketplace, selling items of little value, in order to buy food for their families. And mothers live in fear that at any moment, the sons they have borne and raised at great sacrifice will be forcibly dragged off to the army.

Faced with such a frightening reality, women feel threatened and confused. On the one hand, they are presented with the image of motherhood as something sacred, and on the other hand, they are blocked from carrying out this role. As a consequence of this dilemma, the practice of abortion has recently been on the rise, threatening women's health and self-esteem and possibly causing them emotional trauma for the rest of their lives. The courts in El Salvador do not interfere because they have neither the capacity nor the moral authority to do so.

The alarming conditions of motherhood in El Salvador deform the value of human life and respect for women, and undermine the protection owed to our children. We must dedicate ourselves to resolving these problems. The struggle to establish a new social order is not only the responsibility of women, but of all our citizens, young and old, male and female.

University of El Salvador campus, San Salvador (1985).

Part III

"Your People Need You": Women in the FMLN

Introduction

Fighting wars has traditionally been viewed as a man's activity. But the war in El Salvador is not a traditional battle fought between two standing armies. It is essentially a social revolution pitting poor workers, *campesinos* and students against a professional government army trained to protect the interests of the ruling minority. As women have been active in the popular opposition movements for land, food and peace, so too have they become part of the armed revolutionary struggle for these goals. Nonetheless, as women they have had to face particular obstacles to their integration into the military struggle, as members and leaders of a guerrilla army.

The women we meet in this section are not super-heroines. They are real women: they have mothers and fathers who may not want them to leave home, much less join a combat unit. They have children they love, families to care for. They have lovers they don't see often enough. They have pains and joys and fears like their sisters around the world. They also have a deep commitment to building a new El Salvador—a strong enough commitment to overcome the personal and social obstacles to women's participation in a political-military front such as the FMLN.

The Farabundo Martí National Liberation Front (FMLN) is the revolutionary force fighting against the Salvadoran government and its armed forces. The FMLN was founded in October 1980 as a united front of the five revolutionary organizations operating in El Salvador: the

123

Popular Forces of Liberation (FPL), the Popular Revolutionary Army (ERP), the National Resistance (RN), the Salvadoran Communist Party (PCS), and the Revolutionary Party of Central American Workers (PRTC). These groups are political parties—predominantly socialist—that have guerrilla fighting forces as part of their structure and operations. The FMLN is, then, a "political-military front," rather than simply a guerrilla army.

Each of the five groups that later formed the FMLN was very involved in the well-organized and highly politicized working-class and peasant movements of the 1970s. Many of the women combatants in the FMLN began their political activity during this period, as members of the popular organizations of students, *campesinos,* workers, etc. Aroused by the blatant injustices in the society around them and inspired by the intense political activity of those years, they took on greater responsibilities within these organizations. Many of these women then joined the revolutionary political parties that led the broad coalitions of popular organizations, but functioned on a less public level. The party members developed methods of work and communication that shielded their activities from the government. In this period, the women as well as the men shared in learning the skills and discipline of clandestine work that would make them valuable members and leaders of the growing guerrilla organizations.

Tens of thousands of the movement's leaders, activists and supporters disappeared and were assassinated between 1979 and 1981 by government security forces and paramilitary death squads. Many of the surviving activists, women as well as men, were forced to abandon their public, above-ground activities, and join the guerrilla forces that had been developing bases of operation outside the cities. In this period of brutal repression, the revolutionary political parties began to put greater emphasis on developing the guerrilla units that had been operating since the early and mid-1970s. Many women activists were incorporated into various aspects of military operations at this time. Women were also integrated into the highest political leadership bodies of each of the five organizations in the FMLN.

In the mountainous rural areas of northern and eastern El Salvador, these activists from the cities joined many young women and men from the countryside who had seen their homes destroyed and their families decimated by the indiscriminate repression being waged against the rural population. Many of these people had been involved in the Christian base communities and the peasant cooperative movement. Others had little political training beyond their first hand experiences of poverty and repression, and a determination to create a better way of life. The

FMLN presented them with an alternative vision of El Salvador and a means to achieve it.

While there was a strong bias in many *campesino* families against allowing their daughters to leave home and join the guerrillas, the government repression destroyed many homes and disrupted normal family life. This often had the result of weakening many of the traditional bonds that would have kept these young women working at home until they married. Today, some of the FMLN's combat commanders are young peasant women with little formal education.

In January 1981, the FMLN launched its first major offensive. While the government forces remained securely in control of major urban areas, the FMLN succeeded in establishing operational control over large areas of the countryside. This provided a secure base for the new guerrilla army, and created the conditions for the development of alternative government structures controlled by the local population. (See Section 4, "Seeds of a New Society"). The FMLN's support for these communities contrasted sharply with the destructive practices of the government forces, and led to growing political support for the FMLN amongst the rural population.

Throughout the war, the FMLN has faced an enemy far superior in firepower, an enemy financed, trained and equipped by the United States. Yet during that time, the FMLN has been able to expand the range of its military operations and emerge as a legitimate political alternative to the current government.

By 1987, the FMLN had established a political and operational presence in all fourteen provinces of El Salvador and, for the first time since 1981, in San Salvador itself. Guerrilla units harass and ambush army patrols and carry out economic sabotage attacks designed to undermine the war economy. At the same time, these small units have demonstrated an ability to concentrate quickly for large operations, such as the March and April 1987 assaults on two of the army's most important garrisons.

The source of the FMLN's strength is its closeness to the people of El Salvador. El Salvador is a very small, densely populated country that offers little in the way of jungle or mountain hiding places that have been relied upon by the rebel armies of many other Third World nations. With such a major presence of U.S. advisers and military intelligence hardware, it would be impossible for a large popular army the size of the FMLN to survive without extensive support from a population operating as its eyes, ears and sustenance. As one FMLN leader has said, "The people are our mountains."

The FMLN is allied with the nonmilitary Democratic Revolutionary Front (FDR), a coalition of center-left political parties that works primarily in the diplomatic arena, and, since 1988, in the electoral arena inside the country. Together, the FMLN and the FDR proposed a Platform for a Government of Broad Participation in 1984. It proposes measures to end all forms of repression, to punish those responsible for crimes against civilians, and to guarantee individual and group rights of expression and organization. It also proposes measures that would lay the groundwork for economic justice in the country, including agrarian reform, nationalization of the banking system, and investment policies geared to the needs of the poor. In foreign affairs, the Platform calls for a policy of nonalignment.

The FMLN and the FDR have repeatedly invited the Salvadoran government to negotiate a political solution to the conflict. Three negotiating sessions have been held since 1984, with little concrete result. The FMLN/FDR are proposing a process for a national dialogue, open to all sectors of Salvadoran society, on how to end the war and address the economic and social roots of the conflict. However, the government has insisted that the guerrillas disarm and accept the current Salvadoran constitution and government as a precondition to further discussions. This position has been criticized by both the FMLN and many of the legal political parties in the country as totally unrealistic, and tantamount to surrender for the FMLN.

One of the people chosen to represent the FMLN at the first round of talks with the government in 1984 was Nidia Díaz, a guerrilla commander and political leader within the Front. In the spring of 1985 she was captured in combat by government forces and tortured while in prison. Released as part of a prisoner exchange, she now works as a leader of the Union of Salvadoran Women for Liberation (UMS). Though there are still fewer women than men combatants in the FMLN, the women who speak from the following pages show us that Nidia Díaz is not an exception. Melida Anaya Montes was second in command of the FPL at the time of her death in 1983. Ana Guadelupe Martínez was a member of the Central Committee of the ERP as well as a military commander in Morazán Province. Other women, less well known internationally, have served at various levels of political and military leadership: Eugenia served on the staff of the FPL's Central Command; Ileana was the commander of an all-women's battalion.

The fact that women such as Ana Guadelupe Martínez, Melida Anaya Montes, Nidia Díaz and Eugenia have been active members of the FMLN since its inception has encouraged other women to join and participate fully, and to challenge the stereotypes of women as unfit for military tasks. Their presence has ensured that the FMLN's stated commitment to the goal of sexual equality is translated into reality. Eight years after the formation of the Front, 40 percent of its members are women, including over 30 percent of its combat forces. Women are now participating in every aspect of FMLN activity, including combat, political education, logistical support, propaganda, battlefront medicine and overall leadership. While sexual divisions of labor still exist, the presence of women at all levels of the FMLN indicates that women's participation is not an exception but an integral part of the revolutionary process. Of course, the struggle to attain equality and to meet women's needs goes on within the revolutionary movement as much as outside it. Like most military organizations, the FMLN is not set up to directly address the needs of women. For instance, a group of women soldiers had to organize their own campaign to pressure the guerrilla command to provide sanitary napkins to the women in the field. That this became an issue reflects both the level of women's involvement in combat situations and the many potential obstacles to their greater participation.

In the guerrilla camps women are no longer the servants of men, but their comrades. The rigid barriers that once separated the world of men from the world of women are falling as men and women together face the harsh realities of fighting a guerrilla war, and the challenge of designing a vision for the new El Salvador.

Melida Anaya Montes (*Comandante* Ana Maria), 1931-1983.

Melida Anaya Montes

"We Will Always Look for a Political Solution"

Melida Anaya Montes was one of the most highly respected leaders of both the FMLN and the Salvadoran mass movement. In this excerpt from an interview conducted in 1982, Anaya Montes discusses the issue of negotiations and the political, diplomatic and military aspects of the Salvadoran revolution.

She was born on May 17, 1931 in a small town near San Salvador. Her parents, who were not wealthy, made great efforts to help her obtain a teaching certificate. Anaya Montes began her career as a high school teacher in rural Chalatenango.

It was as an educator that Anaya Montes was introduced to social activism. She was a founder of the National Association of Salvadoran Educators (ANDES) in 1965 and served as its Secretary General for the next thirteen years. Anaya Montes later recalled the union's early days:

> From the beginning, the overriding character of ANDES was its massiveness, its clamor for struggle. Huge demonstrations of 150,000 people were broken up with tear gas and violence. In 1968 we occupied the Ministry of Education and stayed there for two months. It seemed that almost all of El Salvador passed through that plaza, as thousands and thousands gathered to support us.

Under Anaya Montes's leadership ANDES underwent the process of political transformation and growth. Anaya Montes led the massive strikes called by ANDES in 1967, 1968 and 1971. During the 1971 strike, government intransigence led to a hunger strike in front of the Presidential Palace by eight men and one woman—Melida Anaya Montes. All nine hunger strikers were brutally beaten by palace guards.

By 1971 ANDES had become an important opposition force in the countryside, and many of its members belonged to revolutionary opposition groups. Anaya Montes secretly joined the largest of the political-military organizations, the Popular Forces of Liberation (FPL), although she continued her work as Secretary General of ANDES. The union became increasingly involved in the revolutionary struggle, joining the Popular Revolutionary Bloc (BPR) in 1975.

In 1977, the National Police arrested Anaya Montes and other teachers at ANDES headquarters. They were physically and psychologically tortured before national and international pressure forced the government to offer Anaya Montes her freedom. She refused to accept the offer unless it was extended to all the imprisoned teachers. The government relented and the entire group was released.

In the late 1970s, government repression intensified and Anaya Montes went underground in 1978 to work with the FPL. Because of her skills as a military and political strategist, she rose to second in command of the FPL. She helped shape the direction of the developing people's war and became known as *Comandante* Ana Maria. In 1980 she began participating in the Unified Revolutionary Directorate (DRU), the forerunner of the FMLN. Her tireless work within the DRU to build unity among the five political-military organizations helped lay the groundwork for the creation of the FMLN later that same year.

Anaya Montes somehow found time during this period to write several books, including two books on the history of the Salvadoran teachers' movement and a two-volume work, *Vietnam's Experience in the War for Liberation.*

On April 6, 1983, Anaya Montes was brutally murdered in Nicaragua, where she had been working in exile. After conducting a lengthy investigation, the FPL issued a statement which placed ultimate responsibility for the crime on its own Commander in Chief, Salvador Cayetano Carpio. (Anaya Montes's murder was evidently the product of an internal struggle over the political direction and leadership of the FPL. Carpio committed suicide soon after.) The FPL denounced the moral and political degeneration of the man who had been their most respected leader. While mourning "the irreparable loss of their unforgettable *compañera,*" the FPL reaffirmed its commitment to continuing the struggle to which *Comandante* Ana Maria had dedicated her life.

Melida, how would you explain the current tactics and strategy of the FMLN?

The FMLN's strategy is a prolonged popular war for liberation that promotes all forms of struggle: political, military and diplomatic. At certain times one type of struggle assumes greater importance due to circumstances, but the others are also maintained. For example, in the early years, political mass struggle carried the greatest importance; later, strategy was shaped by the military struggle. At the present time, the diplomatic struggle is in the forefront because the FMLN/FDR are promoting negotiations as a political solution to the conflict. Diplomatic struggle is a tactic in use now, but it is also only one part of our overall strategy. Our strategy integrates all possible tactics. At no time will we abandon political mass struggle, which today operates at semi-clandestine and clandestine levels. Neither will we abandon the military struggle.

And if the government rejects negotiations?

We will continue using other forms of struggle, until we reach a favorable solution.

Would you ever abandon the possibility of a negotiated solution?

No, in no way. We will always look for a political solution. But we will also maintain military struggle and mass struggle in all its forms. A political solution is a form of struggle that a revolutionary movement cannot abandon. It is a way of showing the people that we are conscious of the need to implement all forms of struggle, not only military means. Even if the enemy says "no" for three months, or for a year, or for five years, we will always use negotiations as one possible choice within our political-military strategy.

Every revolution takes up armed struggle because the enemy (the reactionary forces) uses that form of struggle to stay in power. The enemy's fight is political, military and diplomatic. The revolution also uses these forms. The difference is the justness of our struggle, the principles we apply and the values we defend.

Do you trust negotiations with the United States and the Salvadoran military junta?

The trust that revolutionaries have in negotiations is founded above all else upon the strength of the revolution, its men and women, and the strength of the people it represents. If the revolution's goals are not met, the struggle will continue in a new form.

Recently, the FMLN has blown up several of the country's strategic bridges. This has provoked media comments that the FMLN is trying to destroy the country. What is your opinion on this?

The infrastructure we destroy is used by the government to move their troops and to transport all of the supplies they need to wage war. They also blow up our bridges—of course the guerrillas don't have any bridges like Puente de Oro—but we do have little bridges here or there over a river, and they blow them up because they know it's a way to make the struggle more difficult for us.

As far as bridges go, we've made it pretty hard on them. Before we began to destroy their infrastructure they had it easy. They came and went on those bridges with their troops and equipment. Today it's harder for them. They are forced to use more helicopters, which costs the *junta* more and also makes the U.S. role more obvious.

All revolutionary movements must take the costs of war into account. We have no other recourse but to incur them. If we limit our actions because we are afraid of what it will cost to rebuild later, then we leave the bridges to the enemy and lose the war.

Would you say that U.S. intervention is the main factor which has prevented a revolutionary victory in El Salvador?

Basically, yes. If the United States weren't helping the *junta* in El Salvador, the *junta* would have already fallen. Of course this isn't the only factor. If it were, we would have to say that as long as the United States intervenes, our victory will be impossible. However, our own development is also a factor, especially the development of our people's armed forces. As we mature, we change the balance of forces to favor the revolution. We will achieve victory even though the United States continues to help the government. Vietnam and, more recently, Nicaragua are examples of this.

The common desire of the Central American people has been, and continues to be, to build a free, just and sovereign homeland. Nicaragua is free! Guatemala and El Salvador are in a mature stage in the revolutionary process. The people are rising up with great strength. We will liberate ourselves no matter what measures the United States takes.

Rocio América

"To Come Back"

Rocio América is a pseudonym for Jacinta Escudos, a young Salvadoran poet now living in Nicaragua. In the late 1970s, Jacinta lived in Europe, studying and working with solidarity organizations. In 1980, she decided to go back to El Salvador to participate more directly in the struggle. Soon she decided to join the FMLN. "To Come Back" is part of a series of letters and poems written to her East German lover following her return to El Salvador. Unbeknownst to Jacinta, these poems were given to Salvadoran poet Claribel Alegría, who was told that they had been found with the belongings of a dead FMLN combatant. The poems circulated in mimeographed form before being published by the El Salvador Solidarity Campaign in London, in 1983, under the pseudonym of Rocio América. Later, after having to leave El Salvador once again, Jacinta "reemerged" in Nicaragua and resumed her writing. Selections from both her earlier and more recent work can be found in two collections of Central American women's poetry: Ixok AmarGo, Zoe Anglessey, ed. (Penobscot, ME: Granite Press, 1987); Lovers and Comrades, Amanda Hopkinson, ed. (London: Women's Press, 1989). The following version of "To Come Back" has been translated by New Americas Press.

To Come Back

You've come back.

To find the city more deserted than ever—full of ghosts, of voices—the joy and pain of memories that spring at you from every block and corner.

You feel overcome by a nameless anguish. What could happen today? You can't even think about tomorrow.

Your sense of continuity in this place has been lost.

It was so different when you were on the outside—waiting to read the news of your country in a foreign newspaper. Here, you congratulate yourself on having survived one more day.

And always that question—"Why did I come back?"

Nothing remains of that past life—nothing and no one. No one who was really a part of your life. Most of them have left, never to return. The others dead or disappeared.

Many people here have gotten married and are expecting their first child. It seems to be the certainty that death awaits us around every corner that makes us want to leave something of ourselves behind—someone who will perhaps live on and continue what we have begun.

You realize that in these past few months you have left scattered around the things that used to mean so much to you—your poems, records, books and posters.

You don't know who to call first.

"He's moved and there's no new telephone number."

"We don't know where she is now."

"He's left the country."

"She was killed almost a month ago."

Nobody wants to give you any details. It seems that these days Salvadorans just want to forget everything.

So many people have died that you wonder how anyone has been left alive.

And running into someone you know can move you to tears.

The walls are so covered with slogans that their message is indistinguishable.

No one is the same anymore. Everyone has changed (war will change anybody).

Or maybe it's you who has changed too much—and you no longer see things here with the same eyes as before.

And the lover that you left behind, what could have happened to him?

You find out that he couldn't wait for you and that he's happily married to one of your best friends.

In everyone's eyes you seem to see a reproach—

I STAYED HERE.

But no one can make you back down and you answer—

I CAME BACK.

You make contact with your comrades—the few that are left.

Many have gone underground or are dead. And little by little you become involved in the struggle. You find that your experience working with solidarity committees is very useful.

But there comes a point when you ask yourself: Why did I come back? If there's hardly anyone left, if working and studying are virtually impossible, if this country is now nothing more than a dark, filthy, dangerous blind alley. Why come back? If the most likely thing is that they'll kill you, or that you'll have to leave again after your book is published. If your friends and lovers have all left or have forgotten you.

They told you it was crazy—an unnecessary risk—that it was just the whim of a little girl who doesn't really know what's going on in her country or what she wants from life.

But you don't give a damn for what they say.

You know why you've come back.

Your people need you now and forever.

And you will fight for them.

P.S. You found your rifle.

December 6, 1980

Eugenia

"They Won't Take Me Alive"

Eugenia's life has been well documented by Claribel Alegría in They Won't Take Me Alive, *a biography which was based on interviews with Eugenia's husband, family and comrades. This book, only recently translated into English, is the source for the following account, written by New Americas Press, of Eugenia's background and experiences in the FMLN. Her final letter to her husband was translated by New Americas Press from* No Me Agarran Viva.[1]

Ana María Castillo Rivas, known as *Compañera* Eugenia, devoted ten of her thirty-one years to the Salvadoran revolution, developing from a student activist into a member of the FMLN leadership. Today she stands as an outstanding example of the revolutionary woman in El Salvador. Not an idealized heroine, she is a woman who, like so many others in exceptional times, put her innate courage and intelligence at the service of her people. In looking at her life, we realize that in the final analysis all revolutions are made by human beings—by ordinary people who must call up extraordinary reserves of perseverance and courage. Often, revolutionary women must somehow raise a family while risking their lives in political activity. They struggle with doubt, with fear and with loneliness—as Eugenia's last letter to her husband poignantly illustrates.

Eugenia was born on May 7, 1950, the second of seven children in a large middle-class family. Her parents were anti-Somoza Nicaraguans who had resettled in El Salvador. Eugenia's father was a strict traditionalist, but made an effort to develop a social conscience in his children from the time they were small. At Catholic high school, Eugenia joined a group of students who regularly visited the slums and charity hospitals of San Salvador. As she cared for the swollen-bellied children of the shanytowns, she developed the commitment to social justice that would shape her life.

At eighteen, Eugenia went to Guatemala as a missionary and worked as a health educator with the Indians of Quetzaltenango. Deeply affected by the horrible exploitation and oppression that she witnessed there, Eugenia became even more determined to understand the causes of poverty and to find a solution to the suffering of her people.

Returning to San Salvador a year later in 1970, she entered the Catholic University "José Simeón Cañas" to study psychology. That same year, her father died of a heart attack after saving a small boy from drowning. This act of unconditional generosity made a great impression on Eugenia, who was very close to her father. She began to work days to help her mother raise the other children and continued her studies at night.

Between 1971 and 1973, Eugenia participated in Catholic Student Youth (JEC) and Catholic University Action (ACUS), the organizations that would produce many of El Salvador's young activists. During these years, she and other students began to realize that the social work orientation of these organizations was incapable of bringing about needed changes, so she left ACUS to join an explicitly political organization, the University Socialist Movement (which was affiliated with a social democratic party). At a meeting of this organization she met Javier, the man who would be her *compañero* for the rest of her life.

Eugenia wanted an even more direct involvement in the social change that was taking place in El Salvador, and in April of 1974 she left for the countryside to participate in the Christian Federation of Salvadoran Peasants (FECCAS). She worked patiently and persistently to organize the peasants of the small towns and isolated farms in Aguilares, El Paisnal and Suchitoto. She shared the terrible poverty and hardship of the farmworkers' lives, and experienced firsthand the violence directed against those who dared to challenge the status quo. A tireless organizer of strikes and demonstrations, Eugenia made a decisive contribution to the development of FECCAS as a revolutionary mass organization. She helped to form the crucial alliance between FECCAS and the Union of Farm Workers (UTC). The result of this merger, the Federation of Farm Workers, became one of the cornerstones of the Popular Revolutionary Bloc (BPR).

While she was engaged in the practical work of organizing, Eugenia was also studying political and economic theory. After ten months of working with FECCAS, she had come to the conclusion that there was only one road to true social change: revolutionary armed struggle. In February 1975, with Javier as her contact, she began to participate actively with the Popular Forces of Liberation (FPL), the revolutionary, political-military organization founded five years earlier. Eugenia's assignment to train cadre took her all over the countryside of El Salvador. When speaking to male recruits, she stressed the importance of abolishing *machismo;* she encouraged these men to take on domestic responsibilities and to treat women as equals. She also organized groups of women and energetically promoted the participation of women in all aspects of political work. The fact that women in rural areas were so successfully integrated into the movement in spite of deeply ingrained *machismo* can be attributed to two factors: organizational principles which explicitly promoted equality, and the determined efforts of *compañeras* like Eugenia.

Javier and Eugenia were married in February of 1976. A few days later, the FPL assigned them new political and military responsibilities, and they both went underground. In December of 1976, Eugenia took an oath to become a full member of the FPL. She and Javier would spend the next five years in clandestinity, often separated from each other.

After almost two years of living and working underground, Javier was captured by the security forces. Eugenia faced the biggest crisis of her life. Her comrades recall that she cried often and worried constantly, but that she never let her sorrow affect the quality of her political work. On the contrary, during Javier's time in prison, she worked even harder than before. Finally, after he had endured four months of imprisonment and torture, national and international pressure forced the government to release Javier.

Javier and Eugenia had wanted a child from the time of their marriage but had decided to wait until they were more at ease with the difficulties of clandestinity. After Javier's release, the couple decided to have a child; they knew that this could well be a prolonged war and that the decision to have a child could not wait for peace. Cognizant of the risks, they saw creating a new life as an act of faith in the future. They felt certain that, even if they died, their organization would care for and protect their child. Despite the rigors of political work, the FPL did not discourage its members from having children and in fact did everything possible to encourage family life.

During Eugenia's pregnancy the couple were separated, seeing each other only once or twice a week. Eugenia took no rest from her usual work and was promoted to the Central Command as Director of Work in Mass Organizations, the clandestine section that directed the FPL's work in the countryside. Her job was to reconstruct the FPL's network of clandestine contacts in rural areas, which had recently been broken up by the security forces.

Eugenia's daughter, Ana Patricia, was born in December of 1979. For the first year of her life, Ana Patricia lived with her mother in a safe house. Javier was deeply involved in military training at the time of the birth; he couldn't risk living with his family, but he came to see them as often as possible. Both Eugenia and Javier made a conscious effort to see that he participated as much as possible in Ana's care and education. Ana Patricia was part of the movement from her earliest days, Eugenia and Javier often taking her to meetings or leaving her with other comrades while they were away on a mission.

During 1980, Eugenia was assigned to the Political Commission of the FPL and given one of the most important tasks of the war: to formulate the structure of a party that could carry out and consolidate a revolution in El Salvador. For her, the crucial question was this: How could the party most effectively provide leadership and at the same time promote true mass participation and true popular power?

This assignment was interrupted by the decision of the United Revolutionary Directorate of the FMLN to launch a general offensive on January 10, 1981. In December of 1980, a month of great preparations, the leaders of the FPL transferred Eugenia to the "Felipe Peña" Front in San Salvador. Ricardo, the commander of this Front, had specifically asked for her to be on the General Staff. This assignment was Eugenia's first formal participation in the military ranks, although she had completed basic military training and had taken part in small armed actions for propaganda purposes. But Ricardo had great faith in her abilities and needed her organizational expertise. He wanted her to resolve serious problems in the structure of the Front's logistics network, which furnished supplies to all military units. As Chief of the Services Sector, Eugenia worked day and night to organize the logistics network that would stockpile and distribute food, medicine and clothing for the coming offensive. She also coordinated the numerous homemade arms workshops that would supply weapons for January 10.

During December, Eugenia and her daughter lived in a safe house, while Javier was on assignment outside of the country. Eugenia rushed to complete her work and to prepare herself to go to the front. Her letters to Javier during this period are full of love and concern for their daughter. She writes of her doubts about her ability to complete her new tasks, but always affirms her conviction that she has chosen the right course. Javier returned to El Salvador and on January 4, 1981, he and Eugenia met for a brief two hours. It was to be the last time they would see each other. The meeting was full of emotion for them both, as Eugenia said goodbye not only to Javier but also to Ana Patricia, who was leaving with him. Javier later remembered that Eugenia seemed to have a premonition of her own death. During their meeting she remarked several times that this might be the last time they would be together.

The next day, January 5, 1981, she wrote her final letter to Javier. On January 10, the offensive began. By this time Eugenia was fully incorporated into the guerrilla leadership. Ricardo, her superior, gave her an important command, placing her in charge of the supplies of weapons and ammunition. Her task was crucial: Return to San Salvador and organize the transport of arms from the capital to units fighting throughout the country. Arriving in San Salvador, she dispatched a pickup truck full of weapons on the 15th. But the *compañeros* were unable to make contact for the delivery, and the mission was unsuccessful. On the 16th, she dispatched the load again, but once more the comrades returned without delivering the arms.

Eugenia faced a decision—she knew this delivery was critical to the success of the offensive. She was not required to go on the mission herself, but she felt that its success was ultimately her responsibility. She believed that, as leader, it was her duty to identify the nature of the problems and to see that orders were carried out correctly. On January 17, 1981, she set out in the pickup with three other comrades. They took the road to Suchitoto and arrived without incident, although the highways were closely guarded by military and paramilitary patrols. But once again, no contact awaited them at the delivery site. Eugenia had no choice but to make the dangerous trip back to the capital. On the road between San Martín and Suchitoto, a van passed them and then turned around in pursuit. Another van, a paramilitary patrol, appeared in front of them, blocking the road. Eugenia and her comrades returned fire and attempted to escape, but all were killed.

"They'll never take me alive," Eugenia had often told Javier.

Final Letter from Eugenia to Javier

January 5, 1981
11 p.m.

My love,

Today is January 5—I feel a great need just to talk to you for a while. There are so many thousands of things I want to tell you that they're all rushing together—words seem inadequate to express everything I feel.

My love, your visit yesterday went by so fast, but it made me so happy. You seemed even more handsome, there was something special about you. When you go, it always leaves such a void, such emptiness. I'm never satisfied with the time we have together.

Sweetheart, I will love you forever. Today I feel your presence in a special way—in me, in everything I do—my feeling for you is so strong. Every day I sense our love growing and deepening, growing like the rhythm of the war.

Gordo, I love you more every time I see you. You must know how much it hurts that I can't have you and our little girl here with me, by my side. Being apart from the two of you is so terrible for me, to come home today and not find her here, not to hear her laughter, her baby talk—it hurts me so much, sweetheart—but I get strength to go on from our people, from knowing that we're fighting for a just cause. I hope all this will be over soon, but there's really no way to tell. I love you both so much, but I've realized that the pain of our separation is small compared to the suffering of our people. We must keep up our courage and keep going. We must be willing to give of ourselves completely, without reservation; that is what I'm trying to do.

Sweetheart, yesterday I was pretty tense and that's why I wasn't able to tell you how much I love you, but you must know that I carry both of you very deep in my heart.

Today communication will be a problem. I know you'll be worried about me. I'll make every effort to be careful, but I must always try to be worthy of the fallen *compañeros* who live on in us, whom we honor through our actions.

I'll try to keep you informed—hope it's possible.

I was supposed to leave on the 7th but they say that the enemy captured "Sapo." The results are still unknown, we'll have to see how it goes. That's why the ones who were supposed to leave today didn't go. We might not be able to leave until the 7th. The enemy has really hit us hard. There's a lot of weaknesses and things that worry me, but anyway, onward.

I'm feeling a little weak, I haven't got much appetite. I hadn't eaten a thing for two days. Today I managed to eat something—I was thinking of you. If I don't eat, I'm not going to be strong enough, and I was starting to feel dizzy. I'll try to get my strength up. You're always on my mind, inspiring me.

The section I'm working in lacks organization and planning. It's a mess—and by the 7th everything has to be ready for us to settle over there. The work is pretty easy, I'm doing alright, but maintaining control is difficult. We'll see if I can pull it off. I'm constantly worried, but at least I feel better knowing I'm not the only one. It's confusing here, but like they say, let's get going and we'll sort things out on the road.

A great big kiss to the baby and all my love. I love her so much. I saw her picture today—she looks beautiful!

I'll take care of myself. But if something should happen, I love you forever—I'll always be with you. Make sure our daughter is brought up as a true revolutionary—I'm falling asleep—been sleeping very little lately—too much on my mind. I'll try to get a hold of myself.

There's a lot of surveillance around here, it's been really bad. We're constantly on guard. I'll be as careful as possible.

Sweetheart, I have to go now. I hope this letter reaches you. I will always love you—a big, big kiss. For you and the baby, everything I am and all my efforts to put into practice what you have shown me. I won't disappoint you.

Take care of yourselves. We'll see each other soon, I hope. Your absence digs deep into me. Just heard some commotion—I've got to go see what it is. Kisses—I love you. I hope this gets to you. I'm entrusting the baby to you. Take care of her, and please don't let her put dirt or poop in her mouth.

Write me if you can, or leave word with the baby's godmother, O.K.?

Kisses, kisses and more kisses. I love you sweetheart, forever and always...

I love both of you with all my heart

Revolution or death—the people armed will triumph!

Your gorda,
Eugenia

Letty

Developing as Women within the Revolution

At the time of the following testimony, Letty was a member of the General Staff of the FMLN's Northern Front. Her story is taken from an AMES pamphlet, From the Front Lines of War, *June 1982, translated by Philip True. Edited by New Americas Press.*

I joined the revolutionary movement in 1974. My first political experiences, my first work with the people, were through the student movement, which in the early 1970s, was at its height in both Europe and Latin America. At that time, we began to press demands of concern to students—for better teachers and improved curriculum. We were also attempting to analyze and understand our society from a scientific point of view. I was studying sociology. My studies and the developments in my personal life, within the context of the growing revolutionary movement in El Salvador, impelled me to search for concrete solutions. It was at that point that the BPR (Popular Revolutionary Bloc) was entering a new phase of increased militancy.

I think that my involvement in student politics gave me a theoretical base from which to understand the larger needs of my people. As a teenager, I witnessed numerous strikes by teachers and workers, and saw the passions they generated in people. In 1972 the issue of elections provoked intense civil strife. At that time, many people still believed that elections could be the answer to the country's problems, but the results proved that this type of election offered no real alternative to the people. The events of those years made me realize the necessity of armed struggle. Even though I was still very young, like many others my age I joined in the movement to build a unified organization, the BPR.

145

The Bloque (BPR) was concerned not only with the problems of one sector of society, but with the needs of all our people: the landless peasants, the exploited workers, the teachers who demanded better salaries, the women of the marketplaces. As someone coming from the student movement, my work in the Bloque gave me a broader perspective on the struggle in my country and my role in that struggle.

For two or three years I worked within the mass organizations, eventually taking a leadership role. As the mass movement was developing, so were the guerrilla organizations. Responding to the needs of the time, I left the Bloque and joined the guerrillas. At first, guerrilla activity was concentrated in the cities: San Salvador, Santa Ana and San Miguel; later it was extended into the rural areas. I became a part of this military structure and participated in guerrilla actions.

In 1978, a few years after joining the guerrillas, I was made part of their leadership. Since that time, I have held a position on the General Staff. At first I was a military instructor and later did political work among our troops. After the offensive of 1981, my duties were consolidated and now I work in the areas of personnel and political education. This work is very gratifying to me because it integrates so many elements within our movement. Much of the weakness in our military operations is caused by a lack of technical expertise among our cadre. My aim is to strengthen the structure of our organization, and to deepen the political understanding of our troops, as well as to improve their technical proficiency as guerrillas and thus increase their effectiveness.

It's been very difficult at times for me to combine my duties as a revolutionary with those of a wife and mother. I was married in 1975, and my first child was born in 1976. He'll be six years old in March. With the help of my husband and family I've been able to overcome much of the conflict between my participation in the struggle and my obligations as a parent. The same problem is faced by many women who have become politically active. I've seen many of them, their bellies swollen with pregnancy, climbing up and down the mountains doing political work. They may not be engaged in combat, but they are engaged in dangerous and difficult tasks. Many times we must spend long periods away from our children while we carry out our responsibilities or for reasons of security. And of course, we are always aware that at any moment we may lose our lives.

My experience has been that the political-military organizations try to encourage and support marital relationships. I have been and am now living with my husband. Sometimes we have been separated because of our duties. I was able to be with my children much of the time when they were small, although there were times when I had to leave them to carry out some assignment or for their safety. At one point, I had been identified by the government forces and was in great danger, and I had to leave them with their grandmother.

Since it is the people themselves who are fighting this war, and since the people have responsibilities to their families, the organizations have been very understanding in this respect. They prefer not to separate couples, as this may lead to problems later on; for example, the husband or wife could fall in love with someone else during the separation. Now, however, the war has reached such a stage that at times it's impossible to keep a couple together, although this is the general policy and people feel free to request an assignment together. But this is sometimes problematic, and so we must accept separation as one more sacrifice to be made for our people's liberation. We are all making sacrifices—the mothers whose children have been killed, imprisoned or tortured, the wives whose husbands have been murdered or simply disappeared.

When I was a young girl, my aspirations were, perhaps, the traditional ones—to become a wife and mother. It was a mistaken concept of a woman's role. Society may permit us to develop in some measure, but it is still within the framework of oppression and the exploitation by men that we continue in a passive role within this structure. But within a revolutionary framework, a woman is allowed to develop and realize herself as a full human being, to be "for herself" as well as for others. She develops her own unique personality, but she also serves something greater than herself—her people and their struggle. She goes from being a woman only "for herself" to being a woman who is part of the revolutionary process.

Our women have learned to combine their duties as mothers, wives and revolutionaries. There has been an understanding in revolutionary men that women must contribute to and participate in the revolutionary process. When there are children, the *compañeros* participate alongside the *compañeras* washing diapers and feeding babies.

People have a better understanding of what carrying out a revolution involves. The traditional view—that the man works and provides for his family, while the woman stays home with the children, not participating in society or politics—is changing. Today in the battle zones, women may go about their duties while men take care of the children. Women are actively participating in many areas: in the militias, in the production cooperatives, in digging trenches and in security patrols. Inside and outside of the zones of control, they carry out organizational work—talking to people and bringing them informational literature.

Within our military structures, women are not only involved in the traditional support activities, such as preparing food (although this is certainly a strategic function), but are also found in high levels of command. There are many *compañeras* in the guerrilla leadership whose opinions and contributions are considered at the very highest levels.

Ana Guadelupe Martínez, in Morazán Province.

Ana Guadelupe Martínez

1978

The Secret Prisons of El Salvador

Ana Guadalupe Martínez was born in 1952 in Metapán, El Salvador. She joined the high school student movement in 1968 at the time of the first national teachers' strike. An activist in the university student movement, she participated in the general strike of Arcos Communes in 1969-70. In 1974 she joined the Popular Revolutionary Army (ERP). In 1975 she was given the position of chief of the ERP's armed forces in the Eastern Zone. At the time of her capture by the National Guard in 1976, she was a member of the Central Committee of her party. After her release from prison in 1978, Ana Guadelupe wrote Las carceles clandestinas de El Salvador (The Secret Prisons of El Salvador). *She is currently a member of the Political and Diplomatic Commission of the FMLN/FDR.*

The following excerpt from Las carceles clandestinas *first appeared in* Revolution in Central America, *edited by Stanford Central America Action Committee (Boulder, CO: Westview, 1983). The translation is by Julie Pearl.*

"This is Josefina, my commander."

Before me stands a man in his thirties, dressed in civilian attire. He has a rugged complexion, which smells strongly of lotion. He seems pale, sweaty and agitated as he looks at me and commands: "Blindfold her and tie up her hands and feet."

Since they don't have any cotton or sticking plaster with them, a private goes to fetch some. Meanwhile, the commander and his sidekick observe me. The latter, about forty years old, short and thin, with a sickly, yellowish face, approaches me. He pulls my hair and forces me to turn my head to look at him. His face has a terrible, sinister look.

149

Then he lets go of my hair and the private comes in with the blindfolds. The soldier puts a big piece of cotton over each of my eyes, around which another starts to wind sticking plaster. When they wrap the tape over my nose, I can barely breathe, so I automatically raise my hands (not yet bound) and pull at the tape a bit. This infuriates one of them, who hits me in the face and says: "Leave it like that, bitch! Men, make it tighter!"

Then they pull my hands behind my back to handcuff me. They also put cuffs around one of my ankles, but leave the other one free so I can walk down the stairs. They start bolting down the staircase, pushing me along, whereupon I fall down, since I can't see anything. I am yanked up and then punched by someone. With every step I take, the ankle-cuff flies up and hits my other ankle, producing a sharp pain which makes walking any further extremely difficult.

I am taken to a place on the second floor—maybe a dining room or a sleeping quarter of the barracks. There I am pushed to the floor and a voice screams at me:

"Look, Josefina, we've already figured you out here. Now we're telling you that nobody leaves here without talking. We've made the men talk, and the same thing goes for you women. So that you can get a taste of what's waiting for you, here comes the first one."

They stand me up, put two ice-cold objects on my hips, and activate the electric current. The shock is overwhelming; my every muscle is jolted, especially those of my extremities, to the extent that I fall to the floor against my will. I'm lying there on my side, keeled over with pain, when the supposed commander says: "Show her how you're going to lift her up every time she stays lying down."

Instantly, the soldier closest to me grabs my hair, which is too short for him to lift me up with, so he pulls me up by my collar and punches me in the abdomen. He gives me a harsh blow, but it is not nearly as painful as the electric torture. Once I'm back on my feet, the interrogator continues: "This is the principle. From here on in, whether or not we finish the interrogation quickly depends on you. Now, tell me, where are Chon and Choco?"

"I don't know."

"Ah, you don't know, eh? Let's help her remember where these bastards are! Give her a long one."

This one is much worse than the first and I hit the floor again. I try to rise, but the current is still running through my legs, leaving them immobile. I faintly hear the commander say, "Enough." Then the electric shock stops, but the sensation lingers. Once again, they lift me up with kicks and punches.

"Well, do you remember yet where they are?"

I remain silent.

"We have to keep helping her. Give her an even longer one—that ought to refresh her memory!"

And another. The passing of the current through the body is so penetrating and excruciating that one feels as if she is being burned alive. "O.K. We'll capture those two, anyway, with or without your help. We've got them under control. But we know that you went when they killed one of the Guardsmen at the Alvarez Meza in Santa Ana. You were there, weren't you?"

"No."

"Ah! But we know very well that you went. There's no use trying to deny it. Remind her of when she marched down to Santa Ana to kill Guardsmen."

Another charge. Just when I think this one is over, a few more follow.

"You mustn't dare to touch the National Guardsmen. Here you'll learn to never bother them again. Good, enough of that."

They are unleashing their rage against the guerrillas, their frustration and humiliation over every repressive body that has fallen. They become savage beasts of vengeance, wanting to annihilate those whom they consider enemies to the death: the organizations that are rising up in arms against the tyrannical government that these soldiers serve.

The interrogation continues. This time they want me to tell them where the arms are kept.

"I don't know."

"Son of a bitch! This whore doesn't know anything, but we already know all about those bastards. Put an electrode on her tits." They place it over my left breast.

Each current jolts me more fiercely than the last, and every breath of air scorches my throat like dry ice. I clench my fists to restrain my groans of pain in front of these perverse sadists.

The shocks continue, as do the questions. They want to know where to find the money and the suspected insurgent bases in Oriente.

There is a pause and the one who keeps interrogating says, "Aren't you thirsty? If you want a glass of water, you have to earn it. Here nobody gets anything without giving us something first."

He is right about my extreme thirst. These prison guards know their work perfectly.

"Let's see if you want water. Tell us who and where Baltazar is."

"I don't know him."

"Well, I guess this one doesn't want water, then. Put another one in her vagina."

This time two men approach me. One of them undoes my pants and pulls them down, then the other puts something in me that I can't describe, not having seen it, but the iciness feels like that of metal or something similar. The jolt makes me double over in pain—but it is more than just pain; it's like a burning coal, an overall shock which blazes through the innermost muscular fiber.

I'm still lying flat on the floor, suffocating, since the tape blocks my nasal passages and when I try to breathe through my mouth, my already parched throat dries out even more. They no longer await responses to their accusations; they just go on naming incidents and taunting me with remarks and electric charges. When they see that I'm nearly unconscious, that I can no longer speak or move, they stop the treatment. They lift me up, and I fall to the floor the instant they let go of me. My mouth and nose are all smashed up and bloody by now—well, my flesh and bones have been pounded against the floor many times.

They know just how far they can go if they want to keep their victims alive. I am left alone in the room. At least three hours have passed, throughout which the radio has been turned up to full blast. They always do this when they want to drown the shouts of the tortured. How many times, in between the musical interludes have those other, terrifying sounds reached our cells—the shouts of some patriot who is suffering unfathomable torment in the hands of the very ones who at that moment were torturing me?

Two men manage to drag me to my cell, where they uncuff me so that they can take off my clothes. Even in the awful state I'm in, these pitiful creatures take advantage of the opportunity to paw me. They lock my feet and hands in cuffs again, then pick me up and throw me to the middle of the cell, from where I hear them lock me in. I have been made into a worn and crumpled cleaning rag, tossed onto the ground. My muscles are all cramping and I have an urge to both defecate and vomit. The electric treatment has afflicted even the involuntary muscles, like those of the stomach and intestines. I try to move to look for the pit, but am unable. So I stay until I fall asleep—or perhaps faint—I'm not sure which.

A few hours have gone by when I sense that someone is opening the gate. Lieutenant Castillo comes in and tells me to get up.

I don't move. When he sees this, he says, "What's wrong?" Feigning genuine concern, he bends down and looks at me up close. "What is it? Have they tortured you?" he asks cynically.

The lieutenant calls in Sergeant Palomo and some other soldiers. "What have they done to this woman? Who came for her?" One of them responds, "They were from the police."

Addressing me again, Castillo says, "And how do you feel? Do you want to go take a bath so that what you're feeling goes away faster?" Then he shouts to the men, "Go to the infirmary to get aspirin, Sergeant Palomo! Bring back some aspirin and water!"

He turns back toward me. "Look, they came to take you out and torture you without my permission. I wasn't here...I was in Oriente."

Palomo comes in with the water and aspirin.

"Help her take them!" I swallow them only to throw them up later.

"Look, Palomo, how they've left this woman. They sure are a bunch of assholes."

The truth is that they had his full consent. I later recognized his soldiers as the very ones who had tormented me. The so-called commander was Sergeant Claros, I learned, who aspires to be promoted to Major. Apparently he is a specialist in torture, primarily in electric shock treatment. Surely he is to be one of the future heads of Section II of the National Guard.

I was very weak for a few days, still feeling the shocks and spasms all over my body. Anything I ate, I regurgitated. Since my cell was cold and damp, I was constantly shivering, yet the internal flames continued blazing from head to toe. The only external signs of the burns were little brownish drops that collectively formed bigger marks on the parts of my body where the electrodes had been placed.

The physical signs—the testimony of so much suffering—are barely perceivable. What can these little marks say about the electric charges transmitted through these spots into the human body? What sophistication they've achieved to leave only a few insignificant dots to show for such a horrifying, scathing method of torture!

On August 15, they raided the San Miguel headquarters and found them empty. A week later, they searched the little hotel room we had, which had also been abandoned.

I knew that these locations had already been evacuated, that the *compañeros* had taken the necessary precautions, and thought perhaps it was O.K. to give the interrogators these addresses. Even so, I knew that I'd been weakened and that I had to boost up my morale so I wouldn't fall again. Above all, my comrades had entrusted me with many other party secrets, and it was my obligation to protect them.

No piece of information, no matter how small or insignificant it may seem, should ever be passed on to the enemy. Because, aside from aiding their investigative processes in that one tip may lead them to another trail, this act implies that they have succeeded in breaking down the prisoner's principles and sense of dignity, which are the revolutionary's only weapons in the face of the enemy's torture and harassment.

The fact that a certain "tip" is useless to them does not justify revealing it. Whoever speaks, collaborates, and this constitutes a strong break in the moral fiber of the captive. The resistance of the revolutionary lies not in her physical endurance—this will be exhausted just in surviving the enemy's prison conditions and all—but as long as one retains her morale and sense of conviction, there is no drug or torment which can defeat her.

My duty was to keep quiet and direct my thoughts toward all those who had fallen in the attempt to construct a new nation. When faced with my captors' torture, I had to remember that the life-long suffering of my countrymen and women is infinitely more painful than that to which I was being subjected. And anything I confessed would only serve to delay this process of liberation that is burgeoning in the breast of our people.

On top of all this, I was plagued with the idea of a possible pregnancy, since a few days earlier, Sergeant Mario Rosales, one of our most despised butchers, had come to my cell at around four in the morning. These arrivals were becoming so common that his did not surprise me. But this time, he came with two men, opened the cell and said, "Get up and take off your clothes." In those days, they often got their kicks from ordering me to strip.

"What for?" I asked. "Your men came in just a bit ago for that. Besides, I'm coughing a lot and the cold floor makes it worse."

"Take off your clothes, I command you!" he shouted. "Or would you rather have two men do it by force?"

It was always this guy Rosales who ordered them to leave me naked. This degenerate enjoyed seeing my embarrassment when I began to undress myself, which I did to avoid being manhandled by his soldiers.

I started unbuttoning my shirt slowly, trying to conceal my humiliation from them and to ignore their obscene comments. When I'd taken off almost all my clothes and asked if that was good enough, Rosales shouted, "All your clothes! You are to remain with nothing!" I finished undressing. What an abominable sensation I had! Feeling outraged and impotent at the same time, I stood there fully exposed. Then the two soldiers approached me and one held my hands behind my back while the other bound them together.

"Leave," Rosales commanded them, and immediately he pounced on me like a tiger upon its prey, knocking me onto the floor. When I fell, my head hit hard against the concrete floor, and I sort of blacked out for a moment, seeing only those little, blinding stars. He took advantage of the opportunity to stay on top of me, until I came to and understood what was happening. In spite of being handcuffed, I resisted him, struggling to get him off in any way I could. Then he snarled at me,

"There's no use in screaming, because I'm in charge here all week, and nobody will come without my ordering them to do so."

My shouts were drowned by the walls, and my voice soon gave out. I was still fighting him when he called in a private to hold down my legs. Two others came in and stood watch by the door. They were heavily intoxicated and the stench that filled the cell was revolting.

I thought that Rosales' little assistant was going to take his turn, but fortunately, the phone rang, and since they were on duty, they had to go downstairs to answer it. They closed the door.

I remained sprawled out on the floor totally shattered, though I'd been aware that this could happen any day there. I crawled to the corner where they had thrown my clothes and immediately covered myself up the best way I could. Then I lay awake, shuddering at every sound I heard, certain that they would return. They never came back that night.

This same Sergeant was the one who had repeatedly barged into Mireya's cell when she was here so they could all rape her. In spite of their intentions, they had never succeeded in doing the same to me...until that day. I have never felt so demoralized in my life. And from then on, added to my worries would be that of his filthy seed being planted in me.

About a week later, when I was expecting my period, I grew more and more frantic as each day passed and I still hadn't begun menstruating. This was surely the most wicked and ultimately base form of torture they could ever inflict upon their female enemy. It tormented me so fiercely that I had only one idea: to abort if I were pregnant. Just thinking about it provoked unfathomable despair in me.

Ana Guadelupe Martínez

1986

"We Have a Commitment to Our People"

At the time of this interview, Ana Guadelupe Martínez was a representative for the Political and Diplomatic Commission of the FMLN/FDR. The interview was conducted in February 1986 by Sandy Darlington and is excerpted and edited by New Americas Press from the March 1986 issue of Frontera News, *Berkeley, CA.*

What are some of the ways in which women have become involved in the revolutionary process in your country?

The presence of women has been very significant throughout the process of struggle in El Salvador. What has happened in our country is that often entire families have joined: the mother, the father and the children. This has allowed the participation of young women, adult women, grandmothers—many types of women from various backgrounds. This demonstrates the popular nature of our struggle, that it is a movement of all the people; otherwise there wouldn't be so many women involved...Indeed, the incorporation of women has profoundly determined the character of the people in this struggle.

I had extraordinary experiences when I began to be involved and we first visited *campesinos.* When we began to organize in the countryside, the *campesino* men said, "Look, *compañera,* let's go to my house, so my mother and my wife can see you and realize that there are women in this too, that they don't have to be afraid. When they told me this, I realized how important it was for me to go to their houses. The women saw me and talked with me and realized that we weren't exceptional people, we were just like them, with the same fears and hopes and faith. Well, in a little while they were so identified with us and with their husbands and their brothers that the ideological barriers between women and men diminished. This has happened whenever there's a woman taking part when we enter a rural village. The women are immediately more confident when they see a *compañera*.

So the presence of women has been important in inspiring more women to join. It's a chain reaction and that's how it begins. Then these women become enthusiastic about helping: they hide weapons, they cook, they make fliers, they buy cloth so we can make flags. They hide us when the security forces come. They do thousands of things, old women and young women.

Do you have any children?

I have a daughter who will be two next month, a little woman! For me it was a great joy to have her, because I believe that until a woman has a child she can't really understand the role of women, or her own condition as a woman and a mother.

The birth of my daughter strengthened my identification with our struggle, because at the moment she was born, I realized how much I wanted for her: clothes, shoes, medicine, a secure future, the chances to study, a sane and healthy environment to grow up in.

In those first few months you hope that your child will be fed right, that she'll have milk, fruit, vegetables. Each time I fed my little girl, I thought about the anguish of a mother who didn't have any food to give her child, and I could see once again how our people are willing to die fighting for better conditions for their children. That is the greatest aspiration anyone can have. The act of becoming a mother led me to an even greater commitment to this struggle, because it taught me so much and awakened feelings that I had never had before.

Of course there are problems, things that are hard to explain. If I love her so much, how can I leave her alone? But she is not alone. I leave her with other families who love her as much as I do. They see her as one of their own children. They understand that if they can't go do what I do, then they can help make it easier for me to carry out necessary assignments. A deep feeling of solidarity develops in such conditions. I believe that my situation is like that of any other woman who works and who has to leave her children for a good part of the day at childcare, or in school or with her mother. Well, it's like any middle-class North American professional woman who goes to work in the morning and comes back at night when her children are already asleep, and who only has time to kiss them in the morning when she gets them ready for school.

…The same goes for personal relations. Like any North American woman, we are attracted to other human beings. We too want to have a mate, to be part of a stable couple, to feel love. Love is an essential human feeling. Nobody wants to be alone or to feel sad, and Latin American women are not exceptions to this. Revolutionary conditions don't make us different from North American women.

There's only one difference. We have a commitment to our people. This means that, from time to time, we have to renounce the concrete happiness of being with our mates. Yes, this is a sacrifice. It's like a nun who decides that she is going to serve Jesus. We have decided that we are going to serve our people.

If, in the course of carrying out this commitment, it is possible to have a mate and children, we do all that, of course. But if, unfortunately, for various reasons we can't, well, we have made the decision and we'll live with the limitations. But I don't believe that anybody, except maybe some sick people, would say that they want loneliness, that they don't feel love. We are like most humans, most North Americans, most Europeans and Latin Americans. This is part of the human condition. It's not special with us.

What inspired you to give your life to this struggle? How did you become part of it?

I joined without really having any developed political ideas, but my family were people with Christian feelings, and my mother especially taught us to love our neighbors. She taught us about charity and sharing, and to feel bad when others suffered, when they didn't have anything and were clearly worse off than we were.

With this upbringing, I was really able to see the misery and suffering of our people, by the time I became an adolescent. According to Christianity, as I learned it, this was wrong. We began to ask how things could be changed, and to question why things are as they are. Soon we began to realize that things can't change because there are economic and class interests that don't necessarily correspond to the Christian life we were taught about.

And so we began to participate in activities we felt might lead to the necessary changes. In my case, I began to participate during high school. Afterwards, when I entered the National University, there was a big student struggle over the university budget. We wanted the university to be open to more students, especially from the working classes. The university only admitted a few students, mainly those from the middle class, who could pay the tuition.

I believed this student struggle was just, so I joined in. We were persecuted for agitating for a bigger budget. When the police beat us up, we started to understand that the people in power didn't want changes. They weren't interested in the well-being of the people. Because of that, at a certain point, I began to participate in the armed struggle, without having any clear idea about Marxism, Leninism or many of the other things that came out later, little by little. All I really knew about were our student problems.

At the same time, another phenomenon was taking place: solidarity with the people of Vietnam. The University of California at Berkeley sent all the universities in the world—at least those in Latin America—an invitation to develop a week of solidarity against the intervention in Vietnam. That's when I first learned about Vietnam, imperialism and intervention—in November 1969—because of the initiative of students at U.C. Berkeley. That's when I learned there was another world of struggle beyond students fighting for their rights, and I began to see it was a very complex process.

In spite of accusations that have been made, we weren't just tools of communism. Our participation was a natural process of realizing the injustices around us and then beginning to act. That participation carried us to deeper and deeper commitments, which we naturally accepted because of what was already part of our consciousness and our decision to struggle. These decisions come because you realize that behind you there is a whole people willing to struggle. In this way, a year passes, then another, and that's how it has happened with us. We began to struggle when we were young, and now we have been organized for ten to fifteen years, and it feels like no time at all has passed.

Is there anything you would like to ask of the people of the United States?

We would like to know how it has been possible for the Reagan administration to succeed in putting such a barrier in the minds of North Americans that they hardly consider us part of the human race. They call us "communists" or some other label, and so we seem to be less than human. So many North Americans don't realize what is happening in our country, don't see us as human beings with the same aspirations that they have. They want peace, justice, well-being, schools, education, work, health and religious freedom. Well, these are the same things our people want. They are the universal aspirations of the human race.

I think this is an important moment to reflect upon how it is possible that the people of El Salvador can be categorized as "communist" and, therefore, as less than human. Most people in the United States don't care what happens in El Salvador, or, if they care, it's not from a human understanding that what is happening here is wrong, it's just part of "politics.". . .So I believe it is necessary for North Americans who still have the possibility of understanding the situation to realize that they may have a distorted picture of what is happening in El Salvador.

Ileana

Leading the Compañera Silvia
Women's Platoon

Ileana was a combatant with the Armed Forces of Liberation (FAL, the guerrilla army of the Salvadoran Communist Party), and became the commander of an all-women's platoon of the FAL. The following interview with Ileana took place in mid-1983 in a FAL camp in San Vicente Province. Ileana's life, so full of promise and commitment, was cut short in the spring of 1984, when she was killed in combat. The interview was conducted by AMPES (Association of Progressive Women of El Salvador) and published in the April 1985 issue of Matrix, *Santa Cruz, CA. It has been edited by New Americas Press.*

Tell us about one of your experiences in combat.

As the day began, 7,000 government soldiers neared our positions here in Cerros de San Pedro. This was in March of 1982. The cordon silently grew tighter. We had just gone through two days of heavy bombing from artillery and enemy planes. We were very tense as we waited for our orders and the moment when we would attack the government army. Most of the civilians, already used to government offensives, had found shelter. Others carried out the tasks that needed to be done at the moment. When the Frente's commanders ordered the evacuation of the area, we knew just what that meant: the cordon had to be broken so that the civilian population could escape and not be left to the mercy of the government troops.

This was relatively easy for most of the combatants, but things were more complicated with the civilians. Can you imagine mothers with newborn infants, pregnant women, elderly people in poor health and young children all struggling to escape the death that awaited them if they were left behind?

The first *compañeros* to move went to harass the enemy's rear guard and to take some of the pressure off us. We were eventually stuck in a 500-square-meter area, and the siege grew tighter with each second. Our squadrons, which were responsible for protecting the civilians, decided to break through the siege in a *"Patria o Muerte"* (Homeland or Death) action, but for the civilians it can only be *"Patria."* At any cost, we had to guarantee that they would come out of the situation without suffering grave consequences.

The shooting began like a thunderbolt near the enemy's weakest section. At that moment, the whole mass of people rushed like runaway horses towards the area where we had broken through. With the intensity of gunfire and the high level of tension, two women went into labor and gave birth. In the confusion, it didn't occur to anyone to help them. I don't know how, but those two women took care of themselves and managed to flee with the others. It is a moment I don't like to think about, and I certainly wouldn't want to live through it again.

Tell us a little about yourself and what motivated you to join the guerrillas.

Well, my family are all peasants and I grew up in a simple home. I got my first pair of shoes when I was ten years old. My brothers and sisters and I had to help our parents in the fields at a very early age. I was only able to finish the seventh grade in school, but that was more than the rest of my family. Some of them finished fifth grade and the others remained illiterate.

When I was sixteen, I was arrested even though I hadn't fully joined the revolutionary movement. (I had done some work for the Nationalist Democratic Union (UDN) after being recruited by two *compañeros* who later fell in battle.) I was held in prison for almost three hours. During that time I was beaten so savagely that I still have not completely recovered. One of the blows left me with a permanent lesion. Several days after my arrest, I set out for this camp with two of my sisters and their husbands.

How have you adapted to life in the camp?

At first I performed a variety of tasks, but I was given greater responsibility as I developed and acquired skill. Eventually I became the commander of a squadron with seven men under my command. My leadership experience plus valid complaints that the women were being stationed only to cover and hold our combat positions led to the command's decision to form an all-women platoon. The *"Compañera*

Silvia" women's platoon was born in December 1981, and I was assigned as its leader.

Our platoon functions as a separate unit: It has its own radio
operator, its own paramedics, and it is stationed in a specific area. When
an action is planned, the command gives us the objective, our position
and general instructions. The rest is up to us. We discuss how to
accomplish our objective, who will be assigned to particular tasks, and
all the details that go into a military operation. As a unit, we have our
own initiative and independence within the general plans of our command.

Our platoon has participated in many operations, and we are now
an experienced unit. Among the most important actions I can mention
are attacking the military headquarters in San Vicente, taking San Ide-
lfonso and San Sebastian, blowing up the Quebrada Seca bridge and
repeatedly ambushing government troops. We also take part in production tasks and guarding the camp. Most of the platoon members are
young peasant women. I'm barely 20 and there are members who are
even younger than me.

I help the *compañeras* do farm work, prepare meals and chop
wood. Working together has helped us trust each other so deeply that if
a *compañera* has a problem, she tells me about it and asks for my
opinion. Sometimes the problem is with a boyfriend, and because many
of the *compañeras* are so young, I try to give them the best advice
possible. Occasionally the men combatants will tease me if I happen to
be in their area. They'll say, "Take care of so-and-so" (referring to a
woman combatant), or "I ask for the hand of so-and-so." Others say, "Oh
no, here comes the old, cranky mother-in-law..." We all see each other
as comrades and we don't look at hierarchy in the same way the enemy
does.

The *Compañera Silvia* platoon has become a part of my—you
might call it my heart. The experiences I have had with the platoon have
changed me forever. Now if anything happens to a platoon member, I
feel as if it also happens to me.

Do you have a boyfriend? Are you married?

I would rather not talk about that. I will say that I long to have
children, but my participation in the revolution forces me to wait until
after the triumph. Some years ago I adopted a child, but he is now in my
parents' care because I cannot have him here in camp.

What do you do for recreation in the camp?

In spite of the war, we still want to be happy and have a little fun. Of course we do not party every day or even every month, but we do have occasional parties where we dance. The women wear dresses; you can imagine how strange it feels after wearing pants every day for ten or twelve months. We also put on cultural performances. Many *compañeros* play the guitar and others write poetry and songs. The *compañeros'* musical tastes vary and there are fans of folk music, ranchero music and rock and roll. TV artists also have their admirers.

Have you ever been afraid of death?

To be honest, I think we all fear death, but there comes a time, especially in combat, when fear disappears and we simply fight to stay alive.

I have come close to being killed. I have even been presumed dead. For example, one day in combat a grenade was thrown only five meters from my position, but luckily it didn't go off. Another time, when I was in the trenches, a 105mm shell fell right next to me, but it didn't go off either.

Once we were ambushed while walking along a path. As we all separated, a *compañero* saw me fall and thought I had been killed. Since it took me a few days to get back to camp, the *compañeros* thought I was dead and notified my parents. You can imagine how surprised everyone was when I came back.

Another time a *compañero* and I were assigned to a mission outside the camp and we had to go through several detention points. Two young people who matched our general descriptions were apprehended. They were later found brutally murdered, their bodies too mutilated for easy identification. I don't know how the news reached the camp, but once again the *compañeros* believed I was dead and notified my parents. I returned six days later, and when I went to see my parents, they couldn't hold back their tears. They had to touch me to make sure I was really alive.

Is there some particular accomplishment that has given you special satisfaction?

Yes. We held a contest in our camp to choose the best marksperson. The competition started within the various units and then the three best shooters in each unit participated in the final test. I came in second in my platoon, and another comrade was in first place. When we went to the finals, I came in first and my comrade was in third place; so members of our platoon took two of the three top places in the competition. This is one of my favorite memories and it continues to inspire me in my daily life.

What do you plan to do after the victory?

My life's dream is to become a pilot. I also dream about traveling all over the world. I will go wherever the revolution needs me, but my desire is to finish my studies and become a pilot.

Roxana

"The Sacrifice Has Not Been in Vain"

The following testimony first appeared in Boletín No. 3 of the Union of Salvadoran Women for Liberation (UMS), Spring 1988. Translated and edited by New Americas Press.

My name is Roxana and I'm 17 years old. In 1979 I joined the FMLN. I was only a *cipota* [girl] at the time, but my brothers had joined up and they and their friends explained to me why we had to organize and fight for a government that would work for the good of all Salvadorans.

Although I was only a kid, I saw how much my brothers and my parents suffered. They were persecuted by ORDEN, which accused them of being subversives for demanding better salaries for farm laborers. So I joined the FMLN voluntarily, went to school, took care of my little brothers, and helped out by carrying messages about things like the whereabouts of the National Guard.

When we could no longer live in our village because of the increased repression, we went to the mountains with the *muchachos* [FMLN combatants]. Right away I began to take on certain assignments. At first I was a cook, which is important work because it provides the fighting *compañeros* with their tortillas.

Later, I was a medic. They taught me how to treat patients, give injections, bandage wounds and give plasma. I was at the front many times and I even treated government soldiers who had been taken prisoner. The *compañeros* in charge always told us not to mistreat the prisoners and to attend to their wounds immediately.

Later, I took a course in military radio communications. I accompanied fighting units and sometimes command units. This is dangerous work because the enemy always tries to wipe out radio communications.

I did a lot of hiking with PRC radio equipment on my back and a gun on my shoulder, but it felt really good to be making my contribution to the struggle that way.

During this time, I told my commander that I wanted to become a combatant. So I trained with my *compañeros*, until one day my commander said, "Get ready, *compañera*, you're on your way to your first battle." At first, I was very nervous. My knees were shaking with excitement.

After several missions, the *compañeros* told me that I was ready to command a guerrilla squadron, so I was given that assignment. This meant that I had to demand even more discipline of myself because, like the other commanders, I had to be exemplary in every way. The squadron was all men, including my boyfriend, but they respected me.

In August 1986, I was in a battle in Usulután, where the *Guardia* were retreating, and one of their officers threw a grenade at me. Part of my leg was blown off. I crawled a ways and then some *compañeros* got me to a camp hospital where I was treated by doctors. But I had complications and we didn't have the necessary equipment, so I was transferred, with the cooperation of the International Red Cross, to San Pedro Hospital in Usulután. But as I entered the hospital, I was captured by uniformed policemen armed with G-3 rifles.

They separated me from the medical personnel who had accompanied me and took me to a room where I was tortured and interrogated. They kicked me in the face and stomach and hit me with the butts of their guns. I spent a month there, under constant armed guard. When the month was up, they transferred me to military headquarters, where they offered me money to turn in my *compañeros*. If I did, they said they would arrange for me to go to the United States. But since I refused, they began to torture me again.

I was locked up there for four days in a filthy cell full of worms, blood and vomit, with a disgusting toilet. They brought me food once a day. On the last day, the colonel came to interrogate me and since I refused to make a deal with him, I was transferred to the headquarters in San Miguel, near Usulután.

They kept me under the same conditions there for five more days. I slept on the floor and every once in a while they took me to the bathroom. While I was there, several civil guardsmen beat on my hands with their pistols, even though I was handcuffed, and they threw me on the floor. During this time, the stump of my leg became very discolored and swollen. Someone who said he was a doctor came to examine me and said I was alright.

After that, they transferred me to central headquarters in the capital. My situation improved a little, since they fed me twice a day, though the food was always filthy. They had me on the floor and I had to take care of my physical needs right there where I lay.

I was tortured and interrogated several more times before being transferred to the women's prison. They never gave me a hearing or told me how long I would be there. They just said I was accused of being a communist. They never allowed me any contact with my family. I was there until February 1987, when I was released with several other *compañeros* and put on a plane leaving the country. Here, in Cuba, I'm recovering from my wounds and going to school. I want to become a teacher so I can carry on the struggle by teaching literacy.

FMLN patrol 10 kilometers outside San Salvador (February 1989).

Part IV

The Seeds of a New Society: Popular Power in the Countryside

Introduction

The people of rural El Salvador have a rich history of organizing to improve the conditions of their lives. While the broad objectives of this organizing have remained consistent, the forms and methods have evolved to meet the changing conditions inside the country.

In the 1960s and 1970s, *campesinos,* under the guidance of progressive priests, organized Christian base communities to reflect on the conditions of their lives and develop collective solutions to their problems. These in turn led to the formation of Christian peasant leagues and farmworkers' unions, which began to advocate for simple reforms to improve the conditions of rural workers. Cooperatives were formed to pool land and resources amongst those who had little of either. When heavy government repression practically decimated the peasant movement in the late 1970s, the rural poor began to develop new forms of organization to continue their struggle for justice.

After the 1981 General Offensive by the FMLN, conditions changed dramatically in many rural areas. The political/administrative structures and military apparatus of the Salvadoran government were dislodged and unable to function normally. This meant that in large areas of the country there were no longer army posts or a consistent presence of troops. It also meant the absence of mayors and other government officials. These events created a vacuum of power in rural areas and stimulated the local residents to create new civilian structures to take the place of the central government.

171

Those who organized these new institutions were peasants who were committed to staying on their lands and who had made a conscious choice to remain in areas under FMLN control. They took on the tasks of organizing a rudimentary economy, regulating production and distribution of basic products, and providing key services. The organizational forms of this work varied from place to place, depending on the history and conditions of each area. In Morazán province, for example, *juntas vecinales* (neighborhood committees) were formed; in Chalatenango the civilian structures were called *poderes populares locales* (local popular powers, or PPLs). What these various organizations had in common was their commitment to addressing the endemic poverty and disenfranchisement in rural areas by building new forms of social and economic relations and stimulating cooperative work in order to create cohesive, self-sufficient, self-governing communities.

For the first time *campesinos* were able to have decision-making power over the way their communities were run. For many, it was also the first time they and their families had access to basic services, such as health and education, which the Salvadoran government has never adequately provided in rural areas. The impact of these changes on women's lives has been dramatic. By making services such as childcare, nutrition and hygiene education the community's responsibility, rather than a woman's individual task, popular power afforded many women the opportunity to expand their activities beyond the domestic arena. In addition, their experiences in the Christian base community meetings and in literacy classes have given these rural women more confidence in their ability to speak out and play an active role in their communities.

Throughout 1981 and 1982, these civilian organizations of popular power grew and consolidated, allowing many people to survive the war and remain on their lands. In 1981 the government initiated aggressive attempts to depopulate rural areas to destroy what it perceived as the social and material base of the opposition movement. Invasions were launched which specifically targeted the civilian population and its food supply.

The response of the popular power organizations was to become more highly organized: they developed new methods to safeguard the population and to secure the food supply, and they increased communication among the various communities. As part of this process, the PPLs of Chalatenango formed a subregional government which succeeded in coordinating the work of the entire area. The first elected president of the subregional government was a woman, Maria Serrano.

In 1984 and 1985, the government escalated its attacks against the people in the war zones. With sophisticated equipment provided by the United States, the Duarte administration began intensive aerial bombardment of civilians in these areas. The bombings and helicopter troop landings devastated many communities and caused great suffering for the population. Many people were forced to abandon their villages and take refuge in the surrounding hills for days and even weeks at a time. While the people were on the run, the army would slaughter the animals, cut down fruit trees, burn crops and destroy personal belongings.

The civilian organizations played a critical role in helping the population survive the air war. They fostered a sense of cohesion that enabled the communities to continue to function, while providing basic services to all. Mobile "backpack clinics" attended to the sick and wounded, and literacy classes were held under the trees. Agricultural production was organized on small plots of land less detectable from the air, and food was shared among the various communities.

However, as attacks by government military forces increased, the situation for the civilian population became increasingly unstable and dangerous. In 1986, the government instituted a new phase in its depopulation strategy with massive air and ground attacks such as Operation Phoenix in Guazapa and Operation Carreño in Chalatenango. The purpose of these operations was to round up and physically remove the civilian population. Large numbers of *campesinos* who had tenaciously remained on their land until that time were forcibly removed to refugee camps in San Salvador.

This forced displacement of thousands of civilians had an unforeseen effect. In their small, isolated communities in the war zones, there had been little these *campesinos* could do to redress the flagrant government violations of their human rights. However, their involuntary presence in the capital provided an unprecedented opportunity for them to communicate their experience. The refugees began to organize and to protest their treatment at the hands of the government. Through meetings, marches and the occupation of the National Cathedral, they demanded their rights as civilians, to live and work in their own communities.

In May 1986, the displaced held a national congress and formed the National Coordinating Committee for Repopulation (CNR). The purpose of the CNR is to organize the internal refugees to return to their own communities and to obtain the necessary resources for the rebuilding of these communities.

In June 1986, assisted by the CNR, hundreds of displaced civilians left San Salvador to repopulate their war-ravaged community of San José las Flores in Chalatenango Province. The village of Arcatao in the same province had been repopulated in 1985, although not by refugees from urban camps. Those who returned to Arcatao were *campesinos* who had remained in the area, living in the hills as "mobile communities." They had decided they could no longer endure such a life hiding from the bombs, and they courageously returned to their town to reclaim their rights as civilians.

Encouraged by the successful repopulations of San José las Flores and Arcatao, 600 people returned to El Barillo in Cuscatlán Province in July 1986. A fourth repopulation, to Panchimilama in La Paz Province, was undertaken in January 1987 by sixty-eight families. The largest repopulation to date has been the October 1987 repatriation of 4,300 refugees from the Mesa Grande camp in Honduras; four separate villages in northern El Salvador were repopulated at that time. In addition to these mass repopulations, many other villages in the war zones have been repopulated in a gradual and less visible way.

While the *campesinos* in these villages face material shortages and harassment from security forces, they are nonetheless changing the face of life in the war zones. Where civilians were once routinely denied the right to live together in stable communities and were treated as military targets, they have now achieved a level of organization and determination that gives them the capacity to rebuild, and remain in, their villages. Now their response in the face of government repression is to remain in their community instead of fleeing for refuge. In the event of an army operation, they will hold their ground and assert their rights to live and work in their village. If members of the village are kidnapped by the military—a frequent occurrence—their neighbors mount a protest on both the local and national levels, with the assistance of the CNR.

Because of the changing conditions in the countryside, some of the structures which existed before are no longer functioning. One example is the PPLs of Chalatenango. Although they played an indispensable role, they grew out of the needs of a particular historical moment which has since changed. They were nurtured and protected by the ongoing presence of FMLN forces in the area. By 1988, however, the FMLN had stopped attempting to hold on to specific territory, or "zones," in favor of a more mobile strategy of operating throughout the entire country. Popular power continues to expand and grow in the Salvadoran countryside, completely separate from FMLN logistical or military support. In fact, some of the villages, such as El Barillo, are within a kilometer of government military bases. Their protection comes from the determination of the population, their "legitimacy" as a civilian population and international support.

As popular power expands through new repopulation efforts, so do the opportunities for women to participate more fully in the decisions and activities that shape their communities. Whether in the form of a community council, repopulation committee or cooperative, popular power exists wherever people are taking control of their destiny and working to build a just society in lasting peace.

Elena

The Beginnings of Popular Power

At the time of this interview Elena was coordinator of the popular power structures in her community, in the FMLN-controlled area of Chalatenango Province. The interview was conducted in early 1982 and originally published in English in an undated edition of the AMES Bulletin. It has been edited by New Americas Press.

We have three main people who are responsible for the overall functioning of popular power in our community: a secretary general, a chief of militias and a chief of supplies. The chief of supplies is in charge of maintaining the food supply of the community, and of organizing the people for food production tasks. The chief of militias is responsible for setting up guard posts, and for all the other security measures. The secretary general is the overall coordinator.

The people of the community are responsible for all production. The guerrillas don't do this type of work because they are involved in actual combat. Their job is to defend us and to attack the government's forces. Our role is to grow and to harvest the food, the radishes, the tomatoes, so that no one goes hungry. Here in the zones of control we can grow only a few crops—we have tomatoes, cabbages and radishes, but we have to buy corn. We've been producing coffee here, so we used the 300 *colones* we got for the 300 pounds we picked to buy corn. When that runs out, we will have to try to find the money to buy more corn to feed the people. The guerrillas have their own corn fields, but we bring our pack animals and help them harvest it.

The women here work as hard as the men. For example, the coffee harvest was done entirely by women and children seven years and older. We not only had to pick the coffee, but we had to dry it, weigh it and deliver it. Right now, the tomatoes are ready to be picked, so I have to go look for some kids to help bring them in.

When the soldiers need their clothes washed, they bring them to us, to spread out among the women in the community. I remember one day they came back from a fierce encounter in San Fernando. They were so dirty and exhausted! Well, they couldn't be washing clothes, so they left them here, and I saw to it that they got done. But the other soldiers, the ones who stay around camp, wash their own clothes.

Women's work here is never done, that's for sure. Maybe nobody takes much note of all the work we do, but there is never a day when we're not busy. With so much work to do, the children can get to be a problem. Now we're trying to set up a school because it's a shame that there are so many kids around here, but no classes for them to go to. We're getting a building ready for a classroom. Now we just have to find a teacher. We've also got a *compañero* coming who's going to teach political education classes for the adults. We really need it, including me—I've had very little political education.

I started to get involved with the movement through religion. In San Antonio de los Ranchos, the nuns held meetings and discussions every Saturday. They told us it wasn't enough just to come and pray and sing songs. They told us that difficult times were ahead and that we must put up a good fight. We read verses from the Bible and the nuns made sure that we understood—they explained carefully, patiently. We didn't live in Los Ranchos; we lived far away. But, I don't know, I liked those meetings so much, that we came anyway. As people began to learn more, the nuns stopped coming. Instead, the people went to other meetings, only for people we trusted. We tried to bring new people into these groups.

At that time, I couldn't read very well, as I'd only gotten to the third grade. But with a lot of practice I got better and better, and that's how I learned. Now we're setting up classes so that everybody, children and grown-ups, can learn to read.

Another of my jobs is taking care of sanitation. I have to go house to house to check on conditions, because a lot of people still don't have proper sanitary facilities. There are only seven latrines constructed in the whole area so far. So I make the rounds every week to make sure people are taking care of their health and hygiene. I'm also in charge of making soap, which we do with olive oil. Some of the soap we make is distributed to the guerrillas.

Another of my responsibilities is the production of clothing. The last time we received cloth to make children's clothes a lot of kids still didn't get anything to wear. There just wasn't enough cloth to go around. The clothing workshop was set up by the people in the community, just like the soap-making workshop. At first we only made clothing for the civilian population, but now we are also making uniforms for the guerrillas.

Because of my experience in the Bible meetings, I help to celebrate the Word of God when we come together every Sunday. We sing the liturgy, recite psalms and read from the Bible. We have discussions and ask for people's opinions of the readings. Later we celebrate with some songs.

The war, and the Salvadoran army, are never very far away, and there could be an invasion of our area at any time. Right before every army invasion, a light plane comes flying over. We call it a "scout." Instead of panicking, we prepare for the invasion. We try to save as many of our belongings as we can. When the army comes, they often set fire to the houses, so we could lose everything—just come back and find everything gone and have to start all over again.

One time, a man from here left on an errand at about five in the afternoon, and he almost ran right into 500 government soldiers who were headed our way. Well, he managed to get back in time to warn us. That night the FMLN told us that we would all have to sleep together in one spot—everyone, kids and all—so we could leave at a moment's notice. Well, it started to rain hard that night and the mortars were falling practically in our laps. The guerrillas told us that they would let us know during the night if they could get us out of there. Women began to make *pupusas* to last for days; we got those big cakes of sugar out of the storerooms and broke them into twenty pieces, giving each mother one to carry with her.

As the day broke, the government troops arrived. The FMLN soldiers held them off for a little while, but there were so many of them—500, coming in from all sides. We fled down into some ravines along the river bank, hoping that the sound of water would muffle the noise coming from the children. Ay! Were those kids screaming! But at least we still had some food left. The rice and sugar lasted us for two days. After that, some *compañeros* were sent to look for oranges for the kids. But the army caught them and killed them. Others came to tell us what had happened and that we had better get out of there fast!

When we got to another stream, the army helicopters were already overhead, shooting down at us, so we had to hit the ground and stay there. Luckily, no one was killed in that attack. At three in the afternoon it began to rain again, and the water began to rise around us down there in the ravine. Then the helicopters came back and began to fire at us again. People started praying, and looking for rope so that we could pass people across the river. And that's what we did. With water up to our shoulders, we carried the children and old people on our backs across that river.

We didn't get everybody across until six o'clock that evening. We hid out in the tall grass until night fell. Then we were brought out and we walked to a little village called Conacaste. From there we traveled to Honduritas and stayed there for six days, more than a thousand of us. We couldn't get out of there, as more refugees were arriving from other towns after another attack. At last, on Sunday, we were able to get back to Conacaste, because the troops had left the area. As our *compañeros* in the militia were scouting out the surrounding area, they had a confrontation with sixty members of ORDEN, who were stealing apples from La Laguna. How they ran when the militia fired on them!

Those were terrible days. For six days we went hungry. There was nothing to eat. But we made it. All of us from our community came back, except for the two who were killed looking for food. Of the people from La Hacienda, some of their young children died—they died of starvation. When we were finally safe, we had to ask ourselves, "What now?" We had hidden a little bit of corn far away, and we still had that. Other than that, we only had a little bit of coffee. Well, when you're that hungry, you make do with what there is—you're happy with just a little. But we sure had a lot of sick kids.

Most people lost everything in that invasion. My family managed to save our dishes because my husband had hidden them in the well. Anything that had been left in the houses was gone. We used to have a big chest here under the table, but the soldiers got away with it. The first time something like this happened, we lost everything, because we had left all our things in the house when we fled. That time we had to start over completely; we made dishes and utensils out of tin cans, clay, anything we could find. But we did it, and we're still here!

So now when the army comes through, we get scared, of course, but not as much as before, because now we've seen that we can come up against them and still save ourselves—the people don't have to die. When you consider how many there were of us, and that only two died, it was a triumph.

In a situation like that, it's my responsibility, as secretary general of the popular power, to coordinate all the people of the community. Can you imagine—all those people! It's not easy—we have to do everything so carefully. The one in front says to the one behind, "We're going now," and so on down the line, until it gets to the last person. We have to do it this way so the army can't hear us. Nobody goes anywhere until everyone knows what is going on. When there's a break in the line, we have to stop and search for those who are missing. My job is to keep everybody together, to make sure nobody gets left behind. And this is how we survive.

Tracey

Popular Power in Chalatenango Province

Tracey Schear is the Executive Director of the NEST Foundation, a U.S. humanitarian aid organization. NEST supports community development in El Salvador through projects designed to build self-sufficiency at the grassroots level. In October 1983, Tracey went to El Salvador to investigate reports that San Antonio de los Ranchos, the sister city of Berkeley, California, had been bombed and depopulated by the Salvadoran army. She spent two months in Chalatenango Province, and the following is her first-hand description as told to New Americas Press in February 1984 of civilian life and community projects in this region. At the time of her visit, the area was part of a zone of popular control. In 1984-86, government attacks forced many people in the area to abandon their homes, along with the structures of popular power described here by Tracey.

To begin with, it's important to know that Chalatenango is one of the poorest regions of El Salvador. Due to the destruction caused by the war, the poverty of the area has been intensified, and there's a lack of resources on every level. We didn't have plates to eat on or cups to drink from. The houses I saw were generally one-room adobe structures with dirt floors. Anywhere from six to eight people slept in that one room, and families of three or four often shared one bed. Some people used hammocks. I usually slept on a piece of plastic with a blanket over me, and I was eaten alive by fleas all night long.

Outside the house, a dirt floor covered by a roof served as the kitchen. We ate tortillas and beans three times a day. That might not sound like much, but it was a real improvement over 1981 and 1982,

183

when people literally starved trying to live on tortillas and salt, or on honey and water, for days on end.

I noticed that, compared to people in the United States, everyone I met appeared to be sick. Many people suffered from recurrent malaria six or seven times a year. They had severe problems with intestinal parasites, and a common cold could last for several months. Now, for the first time, a health care system is being developed in this region, but improvements are just beginning to be felt.

When I woke up in the mornings, I had expected to hear roosters crowing. But most of them had been killed, along with most other domestic animals, when the army invaded the area. Because of this, we didn't eat cheese or drink milk the entire time I was there.

The war was a constant presence in Chalatenango. Often we could hear bombs being dropped in other areas. As we stood outside listening, people would tell me which province they thought was under attack, and whether they had a son or daughter fighting with the FMLN there. I saw U.S. planes flying reconnaissance missions over Chalatenango about three or four times a day. These planes are flown by U.S. pilots, taking off from U.S.-built air strips in Honduras. Whenever these planes passed overhead, the women would immediately grab their children, take their clothes down from the lines and run inside their homes.

Life is very hard for women in El Salvador, harder than I ever imagined, and I think this is one of the things that impressed me most while I was there. All the housework must be done by hand. Clothes have to be washed by hand, sometimes in rivers and streams. Corn meal must be ground by hand daily to make tortillas, and beans have to be sorted, cleaned and slowly cooked. All this takes hours and hours.

Traditionally, peasant women have been responsible for all these household chores. They've worked at home and in the fields of the *haciendas,* and very often as domestics for the big landowners. Most often they have borne many children, many of whom also had to work on the *haciendas* to help the family survive. Because of malnutrition, many of these children die before they reach adulthood. I met women in their teens who had already lost two or three children due to these terrible conditions.

Because Chalatenango is so poor, it's a province where the mass organizations have been quite active. As it was explained to me, young priests began to come into the area in the late 1960s. These priests encouraged people to search for solutions to their problems here on earth, instead of waiting until after death to experience happiness. The people started Christian base communities, which studied the Bible and reflected on the difficult conditions of peasant life. Out of these groups came a very important organization, FECCAS-UTC (Christian Federation

of Salvadoran Peasants-Union of Farm Workers), which organized for
wage increases and better working conditions on the *haciendas*.

The fruits of this early phase of organization can be seen in the
organs of popular power that I witnessed on my trip, in the areas where
new local governments elected by the people had replaced the political
structures of the Salvadoran government. These areas, where political
control is in the hands of the local people, and military control is in the
hands of the FMLN, make up about a third of the country. Called the
zones of popular control, they are defended militarily by the FMLN and
the popular militia. The only way the government forces can penetrate
these zones is by aerial bombings or major incursions involving several
thousand troops. The civilian population of the zones is targeted for
attacks because of its support for the FMLN. The government's air and
ground attacks are deliberately designed to destroy the people's means
of subsistence and to force them to abandon their homes, to separate
the FMLN from its base of popular support.

There are three types of organizations active in the zones of
popular control in Chalatenango: the military forces of the FMLN who
have their camps in the area; the mass organizations such as FECCAS-
UTC and AMES; and the local community governments. The level of
women's participation in all these organizations is very high.

The great majority of both older and younger women are involved
in AMES. Women told me that they hadn't joined AMES before, when
the area was controlled by the government, because to be caught going
to a meeting in government-controlled areas could mean your life. In
addition, getting someone to take care of the children before was very
difficult. Now AMES can operate openly in the zones of control, and they
organize childcare, so women have a real choice about participating.

I was able to observe a number of AMES meetings, including what
we would call consciousness-raising groups, focused on health care for
women. The local community governments in the area were trying to
design a new kind of health care system for thousands of people, and
AMES was working with them to define the needs of women. Traditionally, things like bladder infections and gynecological problems just
weren't talked about, and so they often weren't treated. Now women's
needs will be incorporated into the new health system.

I should probably clarify how AMES and other mass organizations
relate to the local governments. These popular organizations don't have
a vote as such in the weekly general assemblies where everyone comes
together, but their influence is definitely felt. Through their participation
in AMES, women are developing their political consciousness and coming to define their own needs. So when discussions take place in the
general assemblies or when new laws are created, women are able to

contribute their ideas. In addition, the general secretary of AMES in the area serves as a formal member of the advisory council of the popular government.

I saw the strength of AMES reflected in an increased political consciousness about the problems of women. Back in the 1960s, a lot of women's husbands began to participate in the farmworker unions and the Christian base communities. But the minute the women wanted to join, there were problems with their husbands—problems which sometimes even escalated into wife-beating. When a woman found that she couldn't resolve this situation on her own, other women from the community met with the couple and acted as mediators. The result has been a long process of men changing their attitudes and women helping them to change. Women have developed more confidence in their own ability to participate in society, and men have gained an appreciation for the role played by the women. There is a new mutual respect between women and men that rarely existed in the past.

It was fascinating to sit down with the younger women and their grandmothers and talk about these changes. (I actually did not see many women between the ages of eighteen and twenty-five, because so many of them had chosen to join the FMLN. Most of the younger women I did meet had husbands who were with the guerrillas, and they were staying behind to take care of the small children.) The older women tended to be quieter; the younger women were bolder and more outgoing. There was a difference in the way they confronted men and interacted with them, and relationships between younger men and women seemed to be on a more equal footing.

Women of different generations had different aspirations and reasons for working to build the local popular governments. Many younger women had parents in the mass organizations and so from an early age they had grown up as a part of the popular movement. But for women in their sixties, joining the movement had meant a fundamental change in attitudes and values that were already quite defined. On the other hand, they were also the ones who had suffered the most and lost more of the people they loved. They had participated in the development of the popular organizations and had lived through a tremendous amount of repression. Older women provided an important example of strength and courage for those around them. I'll never forget the old woman who told me, "I've had to leave my village at least twenty times because of the bombings and attacks by the army, but I always come back. I want to stay here because it is my home, where I was born and where I want to die. The only thing that could make me move again is an invasion by Ronald Reagan." Hiking and running through the mountains of Chalatenango was difficult for me as a healthy young person, so it was hard to imagine these women in their sixties fleeing their homes and coming back, again and again.

One of the most inspiring women I met was Maria Serrano. She had been a housekeeper for a large landowner. In the late 1960s she became active in the Christian base communities. She later joined AMES and became the general secretary for Chalatenango. Her responsibility was to coordinate the AMES committees in twenty-seven municipalities. At the time of my visit she had recently been elected the first president of the new subregional government, which was formed to coordinate ten local governments in the area. As she explained to me, "We make a lot of mistakes here, because we've never done this before. Every day we are learning how to build our new society, and as we're building, we're learning... You know, I never planned to be a mayor. I never planned to be a leader, but here I am."

Maria and her family lived with three other members of the subregional government in a collective household. Everyone was involved in the household tasks. Women are still primarily responsible for food preparation, but even here men were beginning to help. Maria's husband worked in the local community government as head of the committee responsible for collective farming and food distribution within the region. There was deep love and respect between Maria and her husband; he didn't seem at all uncomfortable about his wife's position of higher authority. Maria's youngest daughter had just started attending one of the schools in the new educational system. Her oldest daughter, who was eighteen, was a medic with the FMLN in San Vicente. Her middle daughter, who was thirteen, worked with Maria on various tasks for the subregional government.

Another woman I met was Isabel. Three years earlier she had discovered her husband's body on the road near her house, where he had been murdered by the National Guard. She was left with only a small plot of land, which she now farms herself to produce food for the hospitals in the area. In this way she is making an important contribution to health care, because in the zones of control, health care includes the need for basic nutrition.

The creation of a new health care system is a priority in Chalatenango. In the past, people diagnosed their own problems and, if they had the money, they went to the cities to purchase medicine—that was the "health care system." When I was there, many young women were being trained as health workers, or *sanitarios*. I tended to think of them as children, but actually they were young teenagers, learning preventive health care for the benefit of everyone in their communities. As one of the young *sanitarios* said to me, "In this part of El Salvador medical care has always been a privilege, but now it is a right for everyone. None of us had ever seen a doctor before. Now we're beginning to redefine what health care is."

The goal of the sub-regional government is to organize clinics in every town and hamlet, capable of serving 200 to 500 people each. Patients are seen by both *sanitarios* and *responsables*. The *responsables* have more training; some were nurses and medical students whose studies had been interrupted when the National University was shut down by the government in 1981. Others were *sanitarios* who had advanced due to their ability and additional training. The *responsables* trained the *sanitarios* in basic preventive health measures, such as building latrines, wearing shoes to avoid contracting parasites, etc. The *sanitarios* also learned things like how to remove metal shrapnel pieces from under the skin, because after the government attacks, there just aren't enough doctors and nurses to attend to all the wounded.

People were also working on classifying and categorizing traditional herbal remedies, to ease the shortage of medicines in the zone; facilities have recently been set up to produce these remedies in larger quantities. Older women have played a key role in this process because they are the ones who know the correct formulations. Rather than saying, "Well, you use a pinch of this and a pinch of that...," they've had to provide exact measurements.

Another major development taking place in the zones is the creation of schools for both children and adults. Many people in Chalatenango have never gone to school and the adult literacy rate is very low. When I was there, adult literacy classes were meeting six days a week, from four to six in the afternoons. Most of the people attending these classes were learning to read and write for the first time. For some reason, I thought there would be more men participating than women, but it was just the opposite. When the mothers gathered at four o'clock for class, older children cared for the younger ones in the town plazas, or in the collective homes.

The children themselves went to school from eight in the morning until noon. In most of the towns I visited, the schools only had a first grade. One of the children told me, "Well, this is the first year we're all going to school. Next year we'll have a second grade and all the new children will be in the first." In the past, these children might have gone to school two or three months during the year, but they had to move frequently because their parents were migrant farmworkers, or later, because of government attacks.

The local community governments in Chalatenango want to improve the school system, but there's a desperate lack of resources. Because there are so few actual school buildings, classes are mostly held in abandoned buildings, or even outside under a tree. In some places there were desks and chalkboards, but often the ground had to serve as the chalkboard, and a stick was used to write words in the dirt. The children used pencils and little blue notebooks during the day, but had to leave them at school so that the adults could use them at night. Books were very scarce. I saw a few Bibles, some books about agricultural production, and *Where There Is No Doctor* (a basic medical text), but that was about it.

Overall, the people in the zones of control face a tremendous lack of material resources. You can't grow food if you don't have seeds and fertilizers. It's difficult to design a new health care system and make it a reality if you don't have medicines or medical instruments. And imagine running from an air attack, fleeing with a whole town of 500 people, and half those people don't have shoes. After three or four days in the mountains, people's feet swell to twice their normal size, and it's very, very painful to continue. For these people under the threat of government attack, having a pair of shoes may mean the difference between life and death.

The shadow of U.S. intervention is a daily reality for the people of Chalatenango. When we hear that the United States is sending five new helicopters to El Salvador, it may make us angry, but it's hard for us to imagine the real impact. For the people in the zones of control, five new helicopters mean that they have to build new bomb shelters, prepare additional hidden food reserves, and perfect their evacuation plans. There is no alternative if the community is to survive.

And these people are determined that their communities will survive. It's difficult to express how deeply I was moved by their spirit. Instead of the alienation that we often experience here in the United States, I witnessed a tremendous amount of mutual support, a remarkable amount of love and deep feeling of purpose in the communities I visited. The women and men I met have a strong sense of hope, because they are making concrete changes in their lives with their own hands and their own hearts, and they now believe in their ability to protect and maintain these victories.

Woman rebuilding her home in Guajirla after spending seven years in Honduran refugee camps (1988).

Mireya

"We Are No Longer a Community on the Run"

Mireya Lucero is a community organizer from the town of Arcatao in northern Chalatenango Province, near the border with Honduras. Arcatao was the first community to be repopulated in El Salvador. The following interview was conducted by New Americas Press in San Francisco in November 1987. Translated and edited by New Americas Press.

How did you become involved in the struggle for social justice?

When I was sixteen years old, I began working with the Christian base communities in the countryside, helping people who had been persecuted by the army. My initial orientation came from women in the Church and that was the basis for my commitment to work with *campesinos*. I first got involved in Guazapa and in Aguilares, where there was a very strong *campesino* movement because of the sugar cane plantations in the area. I taught adult literacy there, using a program that was based on *campesino* experiences. But I was a student too, and I learned as much from the *campesinos* as they learned from me. We had a true exchange.

But my involvement really goes back to my upbringing. My father was a peasant leader. Now he's a leader in the cooperative movement. He taught us the importance of defending the rights of others and of fighting for what we believe in. So in my home, I always had some sense of the struggle. That's really how it started. It was very simple.

And your mother, how does she see all this?

191

My poor mom. She always supported my dad's ideas, but then they captured my sister and killed eight other members of our family. It all happened so fast. My sister was captured on the 11th of January, 1981. She was taken away with thirteen other girls from our village. In February and March of the same year, they killed four of Mother's brothers and one of her nieces. They also killed three of my father's brothers. Then, the death squad came looking for Mother. When they didn't find her, they destroyed our home. So for her, everything was turned around practically overnight.

My father wasn't with her at the time. He was working in another part of the country and so were my brother and I. So Mom was left alone with my little brother, without a home and without family support. It was all a great trauma and she still hasn't really gotten over it.

She's undergone a powerful transformation. When they took my sister away, she joined a committee of mothers of the disappeared, to try to find her. But then the threats...they burned the house down... And that same day they murdered another woman, a neighbor whose daughter had also been captured. So for her to see all this—she could have been that woman...she could have been killed.

It was all very overwhelming to her. I haven't seen her in seven years—if I went to visit her, I would be putting her life in jeopardy. So our only contact is through letters. She's displaced now and living in San Salvador. She doesn't really have any kind of political orientation and tends to be apathetic about what Dad and I do. She's a bit cold and distant and still hasn't really accepted that her daughter is disappeared or dead. She's very afraid and has reason to be.

Can you tell us something about the organization of women in your country?

As I see it, the process began in San Salvador in 1977, with the organization of COMADRES, the Committee of Mothers of the Disappeared. Other groups that organized specifically around women's issues, like AMES and AMPES, also emerged around the same time. They arose out of the university and work with marketplace women. It was a time of open struggle, out in the streets, organizing housewives and women in the markets, as well as students and workers.

Then came the repression of 1979, 1980 and 1981. Everyone suffered, but because the need was so urgent in the countryside, women's organizations such as AMES, AMPES and ASMUSA tended to withdraw from the cities. The main work carried out in the urban centers was that of the Mothers of the Disappeared, who demanded to know the fate of their children and fought for their release. But unlike AMES and

AMPES, the struggle of COMADRES was focused on that one single issue rather than on a broad spectrum of women's issues.

The organization of women in the zones of control and the zones of conflict is the most important for me. It began in 1981 and you can really see the progress women have made. It was important for them to be organized because so many women were on their own. Many of them had husbands and brothers who were playing a decisive role in the political struggle of that time, and many of those men had been killed or captured. Most of the other men had fled the villages.

The women had to feed their families and grow the food, too. In fact, they had to do everything. But along with all these responsibilities, it was important for them to understand why we were fighting and how they could participate in the process. It was a time of going from home to home, from woman to woman, and talking about these things. The first step was to organize educational workshops and literacy classes, because women in the rural areas have the highest illiteracy rate in the country.

We began to prepare women to be leaders in education and in health care. We even trained midwives. The women who were most committed were organized politically, and they in turn undertook the organization of other women in their respective communities. They formed collective clothing workshops, bakeries and small stores—the food production was organized collectively too. That's how they sustained themselves, doing everything their husbands weren't there to do. They were involved in a process that enabled them to find ways of meeting their basic needs.

Of course, there were problems. For example, a woman would say, "No, I can't go out, I have three kids, I have five kids. I can't go to that meeting because I have to stay home with my children." So groups were organized to do childcare. That's how the women began to help each other.

You have to realize that all of this is very difficult in these areas, where there could be a bombing raid or a mortar attack at any moment. It's hard to keep track of all the children. Everything has to be done in small groups that can mobilize themselves quickly and defend themselves in an emergency.

All this was happening in 1982 and 1983. But the first stage of consciousness raising, back in 1981, was the most difficult. Just trying to bring ten women together was a lot of work. It could take weeks, going from house to house trying to convince each woman that she should be out there working in the fields while someone else took care of her children. That was a very difficult struggle, especially when you consider the taboo against women leaving their homes. They were supposed to stay home with the kids and they couldn't do anything without their husbands' permission. So just getting the women to go out and leave their kids at another house was a significant breakthrough.

Now we're at a stage where the women themselves want to be organized. They don't want to be cut off or stay at home alone anymore. Before, they were too afraid even to go to the doctor, much less to get a vaginal exam or a Pap smear. Now, they themselves are asking for IUDs and abortions—*campesina* women who never would have thought, six years ago, that they could do that, even when they believed conditions weren't right for another child. This has been a great accomplishment, and it didn't happen overnight. I think the necessity of participating in a struggle which is our own will make it possible for us to resolve our social problems in the future. That's why we do what we do.

Can you tell us more about your own work?

First, let me tell you what inspired me to get women involved in the struggle. I was lucky because my father was politically active from the time I was a small child. He treated my mother with respect, and he didn't discriminate against his daughters. He always instilled in us a healthy respect for equality and the rights of others, even though we didn't know, then, what equality was or what our rights might be.

As a student, I was very aware of the situation of women who couldn't do anything on their own, who couldn't even go out of the house without their husbands' permission. That's what led me to get involved with other *compañeras* and say, "We're in a war zone now, and women are in the majority here. We have an important role to play."

My first experience was with a group of women in their forties and fifties. This group was the most difficult, because the women had been victims of age-old prejudices from the time they were born. At first, it seemed absurd to try to organize them. I could have been one of their granddaughters! But these women had seen their sons and daughters learn to fight for their rights. I wanted them to understand and accept that what their children and husbands were doing was just and necessary to bring about the changes we all needed.

The next step was to encourage them to do what was needed to support the others and even to make contributions of their own. I remember women who would say, "Look child, I help out with my prayers and I contribute tortillas." Well, fine and good but that's not enough. So I worked with them, one by one, day by day, encouraging them to get involved. Little by little, they began to join workshops and to take care of other children so that younger women would be free to participate too.

Sometimes, I got as many as ten women together. We were in a Christian base community, so I managed to reach many of them on a religious level. I said that women and men had the same rights before God because we're the same flesh and blood. And we all had to participate in the reconstruction of our community because our homes had been destroyed and we women could rebuild them. That would be our contribution.

Little by little, the women began to understand that they were part of a community, and as part of that community they had a right to fight. I don't know how to explain this, because it's been such a long process, but I think the war has taught us that we have to participate and defend ourselves. It's been very important in that regard. Of course the war has negative effects, but it's been positive in terms of women's education and involvement. It's taught us that we can't always be with our husbands and brothers and sons, and we have to do things for ourselves.

The first time we were forced to flee, we talked to the women about why we had to leave our homes. The army was coming. But who was the army? Who was the government? Who did they represent? It was a kind of political education for them. Why did we have to dig ditches or make shelters to hide our things? Experiences like these have taught us to ask questions and to speak out.

I was just a kid at the time, about eighteen or nineteen years old. It was very important to me, personally, to establish a good rapport with the women. The first time someone turned up dead, it was terrible. A woman lost her son. Instead of being overwhelmed, we went to give her courage and to share the pain of her loss. And we helped her understand why her son's blood had been shed.

What about the men?

Well, something that has helped us is that we haven't really encountered that much resistance from the men. Early on, many of the *compañeros* involved in the struggle said to us, "Go talk to my wife because she's making it hard for me to participate. Please, go to my house and try to convince her. Let her know that she can help out, too."

I'll give you another example. I used to belong to AMES. I was part of the national directorate, which was mostly made up of women from the countryside, *campesinas* who were learning to read and write, who were just beginning to get an education. Our first national meeting was in 1984 and one of the women came all the way from San Vicente to Chalatenango on foot! It took her a week! She had three kids, and her husband had to take responsibility for them while she was gone.

He was in the popular militia at the time. Although he had never stayed alone with the kids before, he said he was willing to if it meant she could go to the women's meeting. The meeting was going to last a week and the trip would take one week in each direction, so she was supposed to be gone for three weeks. But there was a major army invasion while she was away and the *compañera* couldn't go home for three months. She would have had to cross Lake Suchitlán, and there were soldiers there in boats. Military actions were being carried out in Guazapa too, so the *compañera* had to spend three months in Chalatenango.

It was the first time her husband realized what she had to contend with at home, because he had to make the tortillas himself, grind the corn, take care of the kids and do his militia training too. But instead of getting frustrated, he appreciated her work even more. Women often work harder than men. A man may work in the fields, but that's it. And if he gets involved in politics, he does that and nothing else. But women always have responsibilities at home, no matter what else they may be doing.

Many men truly value our contributions, especially since we've become involved in the struggle. Women combatants are wives and mothers and assume all these responsibilities. So we've gained a lot of admiration and respect. But I'm not saying we won't have problems later on. We might.

Later on?

After we win. But now, after almost eight years of struggle, things have gotten better and women are in a stronger position. I believe that it is women's participation itself that is eradicating *machismo*. It's also a question of ideology. At least in the war zones, the *compañeros'* political education discourages *machismo*.

Are women the majority in the zones of conflict and the repopulated areas?

Let me give you a little background. By the time the army began to implement its scorched earth policy, most of the men had already fled. The civilian population in the hills was primarily women, children under the age of twelve and older folks. They were the ones who were dislocated and when the repopulation process began, they were the ones who returned.

Yes, we women are the majority because the war has separated us from our men. Most of us are without our husbands or are widows. So we're the ones, along with our children, who have begun the process of reconstruction.

Our real power hasn't been fully acknowledged yet. To think, for example, how we won the right to return! Women's ideas and contributions have been an essential part of the repopulation process, and we are the ones who play the most important roles in the CNR and CRIPDES! It's not so much that we thought of creating organizations run by women, but rather that we were the majority.

How would you describe women's roles in the repopulation process?

Of the 2,525 people in Arcatao, 40 percent are women and 50 percent are children. The women are the ones who make up the *directivas*. There are five officers: the president, and the secretaries of health, education, pastoral matters and production. There are a few men on some of the committees but not on all of them. The health collective is made up of women. In education there are women and men. Of the five teachers in Arcatao, three were women and two were men, but one of the men was killed last October, so now there are only four teachers.

There are six women in health care and the people in production are all women, young women. The same is true for the pastoral committee, which is made up of the people with the strongest religious sentiment. They do the Sunday service and lead Bible study.

So we play an extremely important role: first, in maintaining ourselves in our places of origin, and second, in rebuilding our communities.

What is the daily work that people do in the repopulated areas, particularly the women?

It depends on the situation. Some periods are more tranquil than others. During the quiet spells, when the army isn't around, there's not as much pressure, so we all go about our usual work. We are divided up into collective work groups. The teachers hold classes all day long when it's possible, for both children and adults. Most of the women are involved in the reconstruction itself. They're busy cutting down trees and raising roofs because their homes were destroyed and they have had to build new ones. Some of the women work in food production: gardening and planting rice. They have to keep an eye out for the army to make sure that the soldiers don't steal our crops or plant mines. They make sure that everything runs smoothly. We also cooperate with other repopulated communities, particularly with San José las Flores. For example, we buy supplies together in Chalatenango.

So we go about our normal lives. All of us are involved in one way or another. We work collectively because, first of all, it's the only way we can sustain ourselves, and secondly, because learning to take care of each other's needs is a form of education.

In the evenings we get together and listen to some guitar music and then we talk about how things are going. Does a particular family

need help? Does someone need clothes or shoes or money to buy things?
If a person is sick, someone else provides for her. We resolve problems
collectively, not just the *directiva* but the whole community.

So, that's how things are in normal times. But Arcatao is near a
Honduran military post. There's always a lot of shooting going on around
the border and we're only four kilometers away. They're trigger-happy
over there and it makes us nervous when we're out in the fields, or
cutting wood, or fishing down by the river. There's constant psychological pressure. And every now and again the army comes in by helicopter
and takes over the village. They take our names and make up lists of
how many people there are and how many new people have arrived.
It's part of the psychological war they wage against the repopulated
communities, keeping us under a permanent state of siege.[1]

But on quiet days, everybody is busy going about their work in
reconstruction, food production and education. Those are the three most
important and fundamental things.

Are there many orphans in the repopulated communities?

Yes, there are, but I can't give you an exact figure. We forget
because other families take care of them and they don't seem like
orphans. But yes, many children have lost their parents.

How are they taken care of?

Well, another family takes on the responsibility, but the community as a whole is responsible for feeding and educating all of the
children. The orphans are always with specific people who are like
parents to them, so we don't have children whose needs aren't being
met. The Lutheran Church has a center for war orphans near San
Salvador, where they've been able to bring many of the kids together
and take care of them. The death squads put a bomb in this center last
March and destroyed the whole place. It's a good thing it happened
during the day, because the kids were at school. In Arcatao we don't
have anything like that center, but we haven't had a problem with
orphans. Or perhaps I should say that it's a problem, but it's not really a
burden because we're all in the same boat. We all have the same
problems.

*How has nature of popular power in the rural communities changed
over the past few years?*

Well, before the army invasions of Chalatenango in 1986, the
political structures that served the needs of the people of that area were
called PPLs [*poder popular local*, or local popular power]. They provided
a kind of alternative government on a small scale, and they reviewed

and resolved the problems of the rural populations. They were a strong political force.

But now that we've returned to our communities after having been displaced, we've entered a new stage of struggle. Under the PPLs in the zones of control, the government considered us the social base of the guerrilla movement, rather than a legitimate, civilian population. We were living in a war zone and were targets of the government's aggression. Now that we've returned, we can't be represented by an alternative, popular government such as the PPLs. They had to disappear. But it's not as if we've completely discarded one thing and started something else. The local *directivas,* which represent the ultimate authority of the people in each of the repopulated communities, have the same functions as the PPLs, except for self-defense. So the main thing is not that we abandoned one form of organization for another, but that we are no longer a community on the run. Now we are settled back in our place of origin.

Many people think that the disappearance of the PPLs is a setback, but it's not. It's a step forward, because now we're a legitimate civilian population. The government can no longer attack us with impunity or force us to flee to the mountains. Our right to exist as a stable community has gained national and international recognition. The sister city relations we have with communities in other parts of the world are an important part of this process.

Are there people who never left during the time of the bombings and the scorched earth operations?

There are actually thousands and thousands of people who have never left the area during the eight years of war. But they've moved from one end of the province to the other, like the people of Arcatao, who never left Chalatenango. In this way we are different from most of the other repopulated communities. We were dispersed, living in the mountains, and constantly on the move. This situation is different from that of San José las Flores, for example, which was repopulated by displaced people who returned from San Salvador. Las Vueltas is the only other community like ours, because it was repopulated by people who returned from the mountains of Chalatenango.

Will the success of Arcatao and the other communities inspire more repopulation efforts?

Well, toward the end of last year, CRIPDES made a list of hundreds of families who wanted to return to their places of origin. But the only communities that have been able to return are El Barrillo, San José las Flores, and Panchimilama. The government has obstructed other repopulation efforts because they interfere with their military strategies. But the peace plan has created an opening that will make it possible for the repopulation movement to continue.[2] The people want to go home. But the government puts up hundreds of obstacles. Several communities in Usulután have already begun to repopulate unofficially, the same way that Arcatao did. I don't know Usulután very well, so I can't tell you the names, but there are five communities there now that have repopulated that way. So the repopulation efforts continue and CRIPDES supports them and gives the communities legitimacy. But I don't know if conditions are right at this time for people to march back in large groups the way they did to San José las Flores and El Barrillo. CRIPDES and the CNR are waiting for refugees to return from Honduras before they start the internal repopulation effort again.

What prevents the government from destroying the repopulated communities?

The government can't just do whatever it wants. Well, sometimes it can, but right now it's limited by the framework of the peace plan. It can't just destroy a community the way it did before. Instead, it's conducting an intense form of psychological warfare against us. It sets up all kinds of blockades, economic and otherwise, to make the people so desperate that they will leave voluntarily. The government blocks food supplies, it destroys reserves, it doesn't let the Church and other humanitarian organizations go in. It uses these methods because bombing us or employing troops against us would damage its credibility at a time when Duarte is trying to project the image of a government that respects human rights. The only way to keep up appearances is by waging the war against us psychologically.

Are there aspects of this psychological war that are aimed specifically at women?

Yes. Women from the cooperatives have been raped by soldiers coming through the repopulated areas. In San José las Flores, the first thing the army did last September was to round up all the women and say, "You belong to us." One way they intimidate people in this psychological war is to say they are going to rape "those old whores," referring to the women, or they threaten to rape a little girl.

I was in Tenancingo, talking with the people there, and a girl who looked about thirteen years old followed us around wherever we went. Someone from town told us she was an informer. Does that happen in the repopulated communities?

No, we haven't had that problem in other repopulated communities. But Tenancingo has had more than one case, because it's near the front. It's become a center for what they call "counterinsurgency work." The army recruits pretty young women to romance the combatants who come through there to buy supplies. They've even recruited women to join the guerrillas. Some of them have seduced local commanders. So yes, it's true, the army uses informers. It's not just an aspect of their psychological war against us but also part of their program to incorporate women in the army.

And it's not just a question of one woman. The army has hundreds of women who participate in torture, psychological warfare and counterinsurgency work. Even in the rebel guerrilla front, they have discovered many young women who've joined up, but who are really with the enemy.

How do they recruit these women?

Well, I'll give you an example. The army was apparently keeping an eye on the home of one *compañera* in San Salvador. They knew that she was unemployed and was living off a little store in her home. One day some plainclothesmen came to see her and asked if she would like to make some money. They told her to present herself at a particular place located near a police station. They said they would give her a little store and offered her a good salary. All she had to do was keep an eye out for certain kinds of people, and report everything immediately.

They take advantage of the economic crisis, particularly of people's need to work. They'll offer an adolescent girl a thousand *colones* a month to romance a combatant and report on everything that goes on in her village: who arrives, who they are, how many, who they meet with. So it's easy, especially for an adolescent. She can have money, food and army loans, and all she has to do is inform.

The first thing the army did, when San José las Flores began to repopulate last year, was to recruit poor *campesino* families for "civil defense." These families were supposed to keep an eye on the rest of the population. But people suspected them right away and rejected them.

Did they set up a "civil defense system" in Las Flores?

No, no. The people wouldn't allow that to happen. But they are trying to do it in Santa Marta. The government wants to turn Santa Marta into a model village. So the Ministry of Health has gone in along with the Ministry of Education and the army. They've promised to rebuild the houses there and they've offered people all kinds of social benefits. But the bad part is that the men have to join the "civil defense" and so do the women. That's what a model village is. They offer lots of benefits, but so far the people have rejected them.

What changes would you like to see in the roles played by Salvadoran women?

First of all, I want women to contribute to every aspect of the reconstruction of a new society, a society in which we can discover ourselves as women, as people and as sisters. These new changes are already taking place in the zones of conflict. And now, with the new legal organizations in the city, I think the women there are also discovering this new sense of themselves and recognizing the importance of their work.

I hope, in the future, that women won't opt for liberalism. I want to see changes that lead to a new society. I know it's not easy, but I believe it will happen. The women of El Salvador have won many rights in the struggle for our country, and we will never give them up.

Campesinos fleeing an army operation in their village, seeking refuge in an abandoned schoolhouse (1986).

Part V

"To See Our Homes Again": Salvadoran Women in Exile

Introduction

Every war creates refugees, but the nature of the war in El Salvador—the war of a government against its own people—has forced a staggering one and a half million Salvadorans to leave their homes. The seven-year campaign of state-sponsored violence has produced enormous social dislocation, turning almost one-third of El Salvador's total population of five million into refugees.

Since 1979, over 800,000 Salvadorans, terrorized and uprooted, have fled the country. Two hundred thousand have gone to Mexico, 23,000 to Nicaragua, 24,000 to Honduras, and 100,000 to other Central American countries. At least a half million others have made the tortuous journey through Mexico into the United States.

According to the Archdiocese of San Salvador, another 600,000 to 700,000 people are refugees within El Salvador itself. Displaced from their homes by army invasions and aerial bombings, many of these internal refugees have been forced into the squalid shantytowns and overcrowded refugee centers around San Salvador.

The cause of this exodus is the "scorched earth" counterinsurgency strategy carried out by the U.S.-trained Salvadoran military. A central component of this strategy is the forced relocation of civilians from zones of conflict, to deprive the FMLN guerrillas of popular support in these areas. Since 1982, the people of the Salvadoran countryside have been subjected to the most intensive aerial bombardment in the history of the Western Hemisphere. Documented bombing attacks increased from 111 in 1982 to over 1,600 in 1985. Peasants who survive the bombing are forcibly removed from their land. Rounded up and torn away from their communities, they are not allowed to take their personal possessions, or even locate other members of their families.

The great majority of those displaced within the country are women, children and the elderly; relief officials estimate that over 50 percent of the displaced are children under the age of sixteen. Because the men are more likely to have beeen murdered or captured by the security forces, women are often forced to assume the full responsibility for their family's welfare and survival. Many of the organizations formed by the refugees to confront their situation are led and sustained by these women.

After being forced into San Salvador or other government-controlled areas, the displaced can expect little aid from the state. Government refugee agencies such as CONADES (National Commission for the Displaced) and CONARA (National Commission for Community Restoration), which receive most of their funding from the U.S. Agency for International Development, do little to help the refugees reestablish a normal life for themselves. The supplies that are provided are used to ensure compliance with, and reliance on, government policies. The Catholic Church and relief agencies offer some assistance, but their camps are filled beyond capacity.

CONADES estimates that the number of internal refugees climbed from 16,343 in July of 1980 to over 500,000 in 1985. The majority are unable to find shelter in the overcrowded refugee camps and must live in temporary shacks on the city's outskirts or along railroad tracks. When a devastating earthquake struck San Salvador on October 10, 1986, thousands of the displaced lost even this inadequate shelter. Flimsy cardboard and adobe shacks tumbled down ravines, often killing the occupants. The survivors, homeless once again, were forced to sleep in San Salvador's streets, plazas and cemeteries.

In response to these desperate conditions, the displaced have organized to denounce their treatment by the government and to demand respect for their rights. The Christian Committee of the Displaced of El Salvador (CRIPDES) organizes programs to improve the refugees' living conditions, while at the same time demanding that the government recognize the right of the displaced to return to their villages and farms, to their "places of origin." The National Coordinating Committee for Repopulation (CNR) was created at a 1986 forum of the displaced, to facilitate their return to their places of origin. Since that time, the CNR has coordinated efforts to repopulate communities devastated by war, and worked to ensure their survival once the refugees have returned.

The 800,000 to one million Salvadorans who have fled their country have also faced severe problems. In Guatemala and Honduras, refugees run the risk of being kidnapped and murdered by local security forces. In Mexico they encounter harassment and extortion by the authorities, as well as extreme economic hardship. In contrast, the Nicaraguan government has made some positive efforts to assist the refugees living there.

At least a half million Salvadorans have arrived in the United States since 1979. They are in large part young men from urban areas, although an increasing number are women and children. Many are union activists or progressive students, or their family members, fleeing the death squads and security forces. Others are merely young, and therefore under suspicion of being "subversive," or else vulnerable for forced recruitment into the military.

The U.S. government asserts that Salvadorans come to the United States for "economic" reasons rather than out of fear of persecution, and therefore denies them either official refugee status or political asylum. Between 1980 and 1986, the U.S. government deported 45,700 Salvadorans. Fewer than 4 percent of those applying for political asylum were granted this status. In 1987, the Duarte government pleaded with the Reagan administration not to deport Salvadorans, as the collapsing Salvadoran economy could not afford to absorb thousands of potential deportees. However, the United States has said it will not change its policy, which clearly violates the Geneva Convention protecting those fleeing armed conflict. U.S. policy also violates UN Protocol on the Status of Refugees (1967) as well as the Congressional Refugee Act of 1980. The recently passed Immigration Reform and Control Act is another threat to the status of Salvadoran refugees. As most entered the United States after the 1981 cutoff date for amnesty, they will find it increasingly hard to obtain jobs and support their families, given the stiff employer sanctions imposed for hiring "illegal" immigrants.

Apart from the constant fear of apprehension and deportation, the Salvadoran refugee in the United States must cope with the difficulties of adapting to a foreign culture, learning a new language and finding housing and employment. These problems have been compounded by widespread discrimination against all people of color. To confront these issues, Salvadoran refugees have organized committees in many cities around the United States that have set up programs such as health clinics, legal counseling, literacy classes and food distribution. These committees also publicize conditions for refugees here in the United States and protest the continuing U.S. intervention in El Salvador.

Over 19,000 Salvadorans, mostly women and children, have found a tenuous refuge in UN-administered camps, just inside the Honduran border. These refugees are mainly peasants from the provinces of Chalatenango, Cabañas and Morazán, forced from their homes by the operations of the Salvadoran army. The UN High Commission on Refugees (UNHCR) officially administers the camps, but with the help of international relief agencies, the refugees have organized themselves to ensure their security and survival.

The refugees in the camps are under constant threat from the Honduran army, which surrounds the camps and restricts who may enter and leave. Under the pretext that the camps are a rearguard area for the FMLN, both Honduran and Salvadoran soldiers have entered the camps to kidnap and terrorize refugees. On August 29, 1985, Honduran soldiers attacked the camp at Colomoncagua, killing two refugees, kidnapping ten others, and beating, raping and injuring many more. One of the dead was a twenty-three-year-old man who was shot three times in the forehead; the other was a three-month-old baby girl who had been kicked to death.

The Honduran and U.S. governments have long viewed the refugees as an unwelcome presence in the strategically important border area. Although numerous efforts have been made to move them to camps further inside Honduras, the refugees, with international support, have resisted these attempts. More recently, the refugees have been pressured by both the Salvadoran and Honduran governments to accept "voluntary repatriation." Under this plan, financed by the United States through the Agency for International Development, families are not allowed to return to their places of origin. Rather, they are settled in areas monitored by government security forces. The vast majority of refugees have resisted this plan as well, fearing that they will be used as instruments of the government's counterinsurgency efforts and isolated in areas far from their homes and communities. Many of the refugees in Honduras want very much to return to their homes and resume their lives, but only under conditions that guarantee their ability to live and work the land in peace.

Instead of going along with the government's plans, a large number of refugees from the Mesa Grande camp have decided to return together to their own villages. In October 1987, 4,300 of the refugees crossed the border into El Salvador to return to their homes in Chalatenango and Cabañas provinces. This dramatic mass repopulation was opposed by the Salvadoran government, which does not want people returning to areas where there is strong support for the FMLN. But the refugees, encouraged by the political opening created by the signing of the Central America Peace Accords in August 1987, decided to go ahead. While they face intimidation from government military forces, the refugees are relying on their numbers, their determination and the presence of international observers to ensure their security. Inspired by the success of the first repopulation, an additional 1,200 refugees from Mesa Grande crossed the border in August 1988 to repopulate their villages in the war zones.

The immediate needs of Salvadoran refugees seem overwhelming: they desperately need food, shelter and some measure of security. However, their stories evoke not our pity but our solidarity. Faced by desperate conditions, they have continued to organize and to educate themselves. Even in exile, they are acquiring new skills that will be put to use when they return home; many of the women, for example, are learning to read, as well as to play leading roles in their communities. The plight of the Salvadoran refugees is essentially a political problem; they are victims of a regime that has targeted its own people for destruction. Every refugee—the student in Los Angeles, the orphan in San Salvador, the peasant woman in Honduras—longs to return home and to live in a peaceful and just society. Only with the end of U.S. intervention and a settlement of the war will these hundreds of thousands of Salvadorans be assured of seeing their homes again.

Woman and child outside their partially rebuilt home in Teocinte, Chalatenango (1988).

Adriana

"I Had Never Thought of Leaving My Country"

The following testimony first appeared in Links, *"Three Faces of Salvadoran Nursing," Vol. 2, Nos. 1 and 2, 1985, National Central America Health Rights Network (NCAHRN), New York, NY. It has been subsequently edited by New Americas Press. Translation by* Links.

My name is Adriana Rodriguez. I am twenty-seven years old. I was a nursing student, but could not finish my training because of the problems in my country, El Salvador. I was forced to leave the country in 1982.

In 1981 I was studying to be a nurse in San Salvador, and had the opportunity to help people who had fled from the war zones in the countryside. They were refugees inside El Salvador. These refugees were mainly elderly people, women and children who had left their homes in the countryside and towns around the capital, San Salvador. They were forced to come to the city for refuge because their home towns had been destroyed by army bombings.

I started working with three other nursing students at the San José de la Montaña Refuge. It was the refugee camp that Monsignor Oscar Romero had been planning to open, before his murder in 1980. The refugee camp was in a seminary, twenty minutes south of the capital. We used to take medicine from the hospital and our school to the camp. It offered food, clothing and moral support to the refugees because the government was refusing to provide any aid. They were happy to see us because it meant that someone cared about them.

The refugees lived in inhuman conditions. There were close to 2,000 people, without toilets, without enough water to bathe, without even enough water to wash the dishes and vegetables. The children suffered from diarrhea and other common diseases that can be fatal if proper precautions aren't taken.

Each person there had lived a tragedy. They had all gone through traumatic experiences, such as the murder of a husband, child or parent. They had seen their relatives die after being tortured and burned. Some were the only survivors in their families. They suffered psychologically as well as physically. Seeing this suffering made the four of us realize that it was our duty as human beings, as Christians and as nurses, to help the refugees as much as we could, even though we were only students.

The director of our school, a conservative, bitter woman, called us into her office. She said that the work we were doing was subversive. She threatened to suspend us if we did not stop working at the camp. I answered, "In school we are told that it is a nurse's duty to tend to those who need help. I feel that to be a dedicated nurse I must use what I am learning to help those whose rights have been taken away."

We continued our work at the refugee camp, thinking that she wouldn't carry out her threat. But she did. She expelled us when we had only one year left of nursing school. Since I had learned the basics during the first two years of school, and my friends and I had plenty of practical experience from our work with the refugees, we went on working at the refugee camp.

It was at this time that one of three other students I worked with was captured. She was carried off in a truck by heavily armed men. We never heard from her again. Her mother went crazy looking for her, hoping at least to find her remains. The rest of us were frightened. We realized that the army wasn't kidding, and that our fate could be the same.

So then there were three of us left. One of the women became very frightened and left. Another was more determined than ever, and she set out for the countryside to help the people who had stayed behind when their towns were bombed. I continued to work with the nuns and other religious people who ran the small clinic at the camp. We had medicine, first aid equipment and fluids to treat diarrhea. Mostly we educated people about how to prevent diarrhea.

One afternoon a boy came to us asking for medical help. He said that someone was needed in Aguilares, a little town about thirty minutes outside San Salvador that had been bombed. So a nun and I went by car. We sent medicines with the boy, who traveled on foot through the hills, because we were afraid of being stopped and searched on the highway.

If the army found medicines in our possession, they would have accused us of being rebels.

When we arrived, we found a lot of wounded. There was a baby girl that we found lying between her dead parents. We treated her wounds and helped many others as well. The army claimed that it had been conducting a "cleanup operation" to rid the town of guerrillas. But in reality the army bombs towns where the people are unarmed. There were many such bombings in 1981. Military activity was heavy at that time, and the peasants—all the people—were persecuted, especially in the rural areas.

Another of my responsibilities was teaching first aid in the Guazapa area. That area, which is near the capital, has frequently been the target of army bombings. We left medicines with the people there so that they could help themselves. They called us only when there was a critical case. There was also a doctor who came out from the city sometimes after these "cleanup operations" to treat the wounded.

At that time I was living in San Salvador, where I rented a room from a woman. One night some men came looking for me. I wasn't there because sometimes I spent the night at the refugee camp. Angry at not finding me, they took the woman's seventeen-year-old son. The people I lived with weren't related to me, and had nothing to do with my work, although we had become close friends. The boy resisted, and they shot him until his intestines fell out. He died right there, outside his house. His mother came looking for me, to warn me because she knew they wanted to kill me.

Then they captured my fiancé. We had planned to get married in 1981. He was twenty years old. They grabbed him as he was walking down the street. It was a death squad, heavily armed plainclothesmen. They killed him, stabbing him repeatedly, in front of people walking by on the street. Neither I nor his family claimed his body. We were afraid. We didn't understand why they had to kill him. He was only a student. He wasn't involved in anything. We don't even know where he is buried—perhaps in a common grave with twenty others.

My family, too, was persecuted. My father, who was fifty-two years old, was killed in 1981 in Morazán, where my family came from. It was another "cleanup operation." They bombed the town of Morazán—they obliterated it. After they bombed it with napalm and 200- and 500-pound bombs, the troops arrived. They took my father and some other elderly people away. They burned my father alive, along with eleven others.

I became very frightened after all these deaths. I knew they were looking for me. I had done nothing except help those who needed medical attention, but I had to leave the country to survive. I had no idea of where to go. I had never thought of leaving my country. After all, I was studying. I wanted to be a nurse, to help my people. I couldn't go to Honduras because I knew that many people, as many as 600 at one time, had been killed trying to cross the Sumpul River to Honduras.[1] Others had been killed fleeing to Nicaragua. So I went to Guatemala. But I felt just as insecure there. With the little money I had left, I went to Mexico with a dozen other Salvadorans who were in the same situation.

When we arrived in Mexico we didn't know what to do. We rented a single room for all of us and started looking for jobs. None of us could find anything. Life in Mexico is very hard, especially for women, which probably explains the high rate of prostitution.

I had a distant cousin living in Texas. I called him to ask him for help, for money. He said the only thing I could do was to come to the United States. He sent me money for a "coyote"—that's a guide across the border. But I didn't know how to find one. Finally I found someone, a Texan, who said he would take me across. It took ten days. We had to walk for five nights. It was raining and our feet were covered with sores. When we crossed the river, I lost my grip and might have drowned if the "coyote" hadn't saved me.

After a year in this country, I began to work with the Committee of Central American Refugees (CRECEN). I still wanted to be a nurse, and they told me there was a health project, a clinic, where I could work. I worked there for a year, and then moved on to Long Island, New York, to work on a similar project—establishing a clinic there for refugees. I know the problems refugees have getting documents and social services. The other nurses who worked in the clinic were all basically in the same situation. We had all been threatened and had to leave our country. One had been in Costa Rica for a while, but conditions for refugees there were very bad—they were closely watched—and so she finally came here. Another had been threatened because she operated a private clinic out of her house, giving injections and so on, which attracted the attention of the authorities, who assumed she was taking care of guerrillas. Another nurse was forced to flee El Salvador, and now works here in a home for the elderly.

None of us is able to practice nursing. I have to clean houses to earn money. I'd like to resume nursing studies, but I'm undocumented and don't speak much English. The Sanctuary Movement[2] can help me find work and help with other problems, like getting medicine, but they can't get me a visa. They told me that if I'm picked up they will fight against my deportation. They know that the same thing will happen to me that has happened to others who have been deported. Santana Chirino Amaya, a Salvadoran, was deported a year ago and murdered within a month of his arrival in El Salvador. There are many cases like this.

CRECEN is working to get political refugee status for us. After all, we are political refugees. We left our country because of the war, because it's dangerous to live in the middle of a war, even if one is not actively participating in it. Providing health care to people who need it the most is a crime in El Salvador. It is because of the war that we had to leave.

That makes us political refugees.

Teresa

"Vision of a Life Free from Terror"

The following interview was conducted in 1983, in Managua, Nicaragua, where Teresa was working for the AMES National Commission on Refugees. It was recorded and translated by Susan Hansell for New Americas Press.

Tell us how you came to live in Nicaragua.

Teresa is not my real name. For security reasons I don't use my real name. I am twenty-four years old. I came to Nicaragua in July 1981 with my parents, my brothers and sisters, and my three-year-old son. I left El Salvador because to live there means living with the horrors and difficulties of war.

In my village in El Salvador, we were all organized into the FTC (Federation of Farmworkers). We were opposed to the power structure that exists in our country, and we were working every day to build a popular movement.

If I had stayed, I would has been persecuted as my husband was. One day they captured him and he just disappeared. I don't know what happened to him. I heard various reports, but nothing concrete. Someone told me they had seen him in the National Police prison. Someone else said they thought they had seen his body. But none of these reports have been confirmed. So I don't really know where he is. I only know he is gone. He was an organizer with the FTC, and he fought for the day when we will have a government that holds the interests of the workers in its heart. He was working to realize our vision of a life free from terror, a life of peace.

The day my husband was taken, thousands of soldiers came into our village. They robbed us, took everything we had, and then they burned our houses. They seized a *compañera* and tortured her for hours, tearing her body apart piece by piece. Then they poured gasoline over her and burned her, as a warning to the rest of us. Later they captured several more *compañeras,* including my sister. They tortured them for three or four hours, and then killed them. My husband was among the many other people they captured that day.

We were all there when this happened, but what could we do? We weren't prepared for such a massive attack. I fled with my family. We went from village to village, living in one house for a few months, then leaving again and going to another. Three months here, three months there, until we ran out of money. We couldn't pay for housing, and we had nothing to live on. We had to leave our country as refugees. That's when we came to Nicaragua.

What kind of work were you doing before you left?

I worked in the harvests and I sewed ready-made clothes. It was all piece work. I was also organizing in the FTC. At first I was part of the rank and file. Little by little, I was given more important tasks, and eventually I became a member of the National Commission of the FTC. I wasn't in the Commission for very long, but I learned a lot from the experience.

Forgive me, but I have to speak vaguely to protect my identity. We are always afraid of encountering the enemy, wherever we are. But I want to make it clear that my experiences are very common to the women, to all the people, of El Salvador. We've all suffered so much. There are many women who have suffered the same tragedies. Oh, the stories I could tell you! Here in Managua, I've met women who once had large extended families, but they have lost their husbands and all of their children in the war. Now they are completely alone.

The pain we have suffered is a great weight we always carry with us. I'm lucky; I still have my parents, most of my brothers and sisters and my son. The women I know who have stayed in El Salvador have a spirit that is so strong and courageous. They continue to confront the enemy, and now they are better organized and better armed. But I became weak, and that is another reason why I left.

What kind of work are you doing now?

Now I work with AMES in Managua. We help to meet the needs of the refugees living here. I visit them, orient them to their new environment and bring them news from El Salvador so they won't feel so isolated. There are many refugees here in Nicaragua who do not live in refugee camps. They live in houses just like this one. We are all homesick and want very much to return to our country.

To the North American *compañeras* who will be reading about my life, I want to say thank you for this opportunity to speak. I hope that one day, not too far off, we can meet each other in a free El Salvador. It is possible that our triumph may happen in the not-too-distant future, but the U.S. government is intervening to try to destroy our movement. We will not be able to stop the destruction of El Salvador without the help of the *compañeras* in the United States. Our future depends on you.

La Virtud refugee center, Honduras (1981).

Eva

"To See Our Homes Again"

The following interview was conducted in 1983 by an international relief agency worker stationed in Mesa Grande refugee camp. Translated and edited by New Americas Press.

Tell us about your work in El Salvador.

My work in El Salvador was the work of the poor people in the countryside—grinding corn, doing housework and taking breakfast out to the workers in the cornfields. At the same time, I had to help my parents out. I only went as far as the third grade in school. Then I had to quit because there wasn't enough money for my education and there weren't enough teachers in our area.

How is life different here in Mesa Grande?

Well, we've learned some important things that we didn't know in El Salvador—about health, for example. First there was one doctor here in the camp, then some of the refugees trained with him, and now they're serving our community. We trust these health workers completely—they can take care of people as well as the doctors can. It makes us happy to know that there are people among us who can help when we're sick. We're learning about nutrition too. Now there's a group of us, a class, learning what the body needs to develop and how vitamins protect the body against disease. And other things we've developed here—the shoe shop, the hammock-making workshop, the tailoring workshop—all these skills will help us in the future.

I've been sewing clothes for the people in the camp. This is the first time I've worked in a shop like this. I'm also doing a lot of pastoral work here among the refugees. I try to help people in any way I can.

With all of this, I don't have much time to rest, but I do my work with joy in my heart.

Although we were very active in El Salvador, our pastoral work has grown quite a bit here in Mesa Grande. It's important now because our Christian community gives us strength. Our faith helps us to keep up our efforts in the camp. Here we have catechists, Delegates of the Word and one pastoral leader per camp. There's one Christian base community for every ten tents. We hold prayer meetings with the people of each base community to talk about the Gospel, about how our lives should be and about how we can improve our lives here. We pray that God will give us the strength to help ourselves—this is the only hope we have. God tells us that wherever there is a suffering person, there He is as well.

To us, a Christian base community is a group of people in unity, with love and equality for everyone. The man or woman who loves and serves others becomes a Christ, at one with the Trinity. And so God invites us to be a united community. We must not be indifferent to the sufferings of others. We are brothers and sisters, and we must feel what our brothers and sisters feel, and share what we have with them.

How do you help the children understand what happened in the past, and why they can't go back to their homes now?

It's very hard to explain these things, but when they ask us, "Where's my father?" we have to tell them, "He died." Then they ask us, "Why did he die?" and we tell them, "He died because of the repression. He was killed by those who don't respect the rights of poor people like us." They ask, "Where's my mother?" and we answer with sorrow, "They killed her." "Why? What did my mother do?" And we have to reply, "Nothing." They can't understand what they've done to deserve having their parents taken away from them.

The children often ask us, "When can we go back to our little house?" We don't have the heart to tell them that our houses might not be there when we return, so we tell them, "Maybe next year." They're always saying, "Come on, let's go now. We can't stand it in this camp anymore. Let's go out to the countryside." That's because here in the camp, they're only allowed to go from their tents to the schoolhouse.

The rest of us often feel just like the children. We can only go from our tents to our work and back again, and all the time we're thinking, "When will we be free? When will we be able to enjoy ourselves again?" This sadness is with us all the time. We feel better being at work, because then we don't have to spend all our time in the tents. Our hard work distracts us. We want so much to be free to return to El Salvador, to be with the friends and family we left there, to see our homes again. But we cannot go back right now, so we ask to be able to stay here in Mesa

Grande, until the time is right for us to return to our country. We have worked so hard here to better our lives. Sometimes we feel over- whelmed, but God helps us in our sorrow. Surely our suffering and our efforts here mean something.

Mesa Grande refugee camp, Honduras (1987).

Maritza

"We Want Our Desires To Be Respected"

The following interview was conducted in 1984 by an international relief worker in the Mesa Grande refugee camp. Translated and edited by New Americas Press.

What do you do at Mesa Grande?

My name is Maritza and I come from the department of Chalatenango. I was a housewife there. I lived too far from town to do any other kind of work. Here things are different, because there are many areas to work in. Right now, I'm working as a supplies coordinator. There's a coordinator for every ten tents; we distribute things from the communal warehouse. These goods are produced by people here in the camp, and they're distributed by the coordinators according to the needs of the people in each group of tents. Those who are more in need receive extra goods.

How are the children being raised here? What are the differences between family life here and in El Salvador?

Well, it was different in El Salvador. It was harder to raise our children there. In El Salvador, when the children were sick, there was no place to take them—no health center. If you did manage to get them to a clinic, you'd get a lecture about how to feed your kids. But what's the point if you don't even have enough money to buy food for your kids? Here, when a child is sick, the healthworker comes around and gives you a note to take the child to the clinic, where she can get attention and medicine. Also, the children have been better nourished here, at least until the milk supplement program and nutrition center were closed down. We were beginning to feel much better about our children's health, but now it looks as if they're getting skinny again.

Education is much better here than back home. Here the children attend preschool from three years old until they're seven. Then they go to first grade, and on from there according to their ability and interests. In El Salvador teachers weren't sent out to the rural areas, and education was very poor, but here all the children can go to school.

How do you explain to the children why they had to leave El Salvador and come to the refugee camp?

Well, some of the children are old enough to understand. They'll ask where their father is, or what happened to the rest of their family. It's very sad to have to explain to them why they're here, but it's a reality, and we can't deny the truth to our children. We're here because we protested against the exploitation, misery and hunger caused by the Fourteen Families[3] in our country, and for this we were massacred and forced to leave our homes. That's why we're here, forced to live as refugees in this strange place, forcibly separated from our families and friends.

How do people here feel about the planned relocation?[4]

We're against it. When we were moved before from La Virtud,[5] they promised to protect our lives; they promised that they would not move us again. We've been here now for two and a half years and have just barely finished constructing the camp. The work was so hard and we want our labor to be valued and our desires to be respected. A new camp means constructing new streets, new water tanks, new houses. We remember how it was when we first arrived here, before the camp was built: our children exposed to rain and all sorts of weather. If we relocate, it will be the same all over again—we will suffer and expend our energy and then be moved again.

They are promising us land, but we're not interested. We want to return to our own country. If there is arable land in Olanchito to give to us, it should be given to the peasants there. And Olanchito is farther into the interior of Honduras. Moving there would make it even harder for us to return to El Salvador. It would mean that none of our relatives could visit us, because of the distance, and it would be much harder for those fleeing the repression in El Salvador to find refuge. Also, Olanchito is right near the largest military bases in the country, and we're afraid there would be more of the repression we've already experienced from the Honduran military. They'll have much more control over us at Olanchito. If they're promising protection, let them provide it right here where we are. We need protection, not relocation.

What do you think about the presence of so many U.S. military personnel in Honduras?

We ask that the U.S. government stop all military aid to both Honduras and El Salvador. The planes, weapons and troops that they send create more bloodshed throughout Central America. The Honduran government presents a "democratic" image to the world, but within Honduras it's clear that they're directly allied with the Reagan government and support the "gringo" troops who have set up landing strips here to intervene more directly in El Salvador. We demand an end to that intervention.

How do you see the future for yourselves and your families?

With all the aid being sent by the U.S. government, the future that we long for seems further away every day. The only solution to our situation, the only way we can return home and live in peace, is for the U.S. and Salvadoran governments to agree to a dialogue. The government in El Salvador now is not a democratic government—the corpses of murdered people are still showing up every day.

We want to return to our country as soon as possible and share what we've learned here in the camps. But we want to return to a country at peace, without the repression that made us leave in the first place. We want a future with better conditions for us and for our children, where we can live without fear of persecution. No more exploiters and exploited. We will work, of course, but we will all share equally. We want to be the ones that benefit from our work. Most of us refugees were peasants in El Salvador, and we want to be able to live in peace and tranquility.

Woman who has been forced to move twice by war and once by the earthquake, at a temporary shelter for the displaced outside San Salvador (1986).

Bettina

"Sadness, Happiness and Hope"

Bettina Koepke is a German medical doctor who worked at the Colomoncagua refugee camp in Honduras for six months. This testimony first appeared in Forced To Move: Salvadoran Refugees in Honduras, *by Renato Camarda (San Francisco, CA: Solidarity Publications, 1985).*

From January to July of 1983 I worked as a doctor in the refugee camp at Colomoncagua. Parting at the end was not easy. I was crying and the refugees were too, and although it was difficult for me to explain why I had to leave, they understood and accepted it.

Until I left the camp, I hadn't realized that I had developed such close personal relationships with many of the refugees. I had respected them greatly for the way in which they managed their lives, for everything they had suffered. They also had respect for me, and so it was an open friendship.

In Germany, the situation is more complicated. It's more difficult to locate the fundamental problems. The most important ones. In Germany, people often worry about superficial things. In the refugee camps, life is different; there are so many tensions. It's so hard not to be able to go out, to be surrounded by soldiers, to have such problems in getting water and firewood. But the refugees have such strength, and such a great desire to survive and to improve their situation. This has given me tremendous hope, because I see there are possibilities of living life differently from the way it is in Germany.

What I mean is that the refugees are peasants and they don't have much of an education, but they have all made the decision to learn, to change their lives, and to end their sufferings. They have made this decision in a very simple way, without pride, humble, but happy with their decision.

Of course, when I came here I knew something about the determination of the Salvadoran peasants, and about the persecution they suffered in El Salvador and Honduras. But to have seen them in reality, living together in the camps with thirty people in one tent, trying to organize their lives and find solutions to their problems, this is something that has made a great impression on me. It was an important and incredible experience for me.

I remember the case of a health worker, a woman with a very strong character. I arrived at the clinic tent one morning and found her crying. She told me she was having problems with her husband, that he had another woman. This is something quite common among the men and women in the camps.

So the health worker asked for a meeting with the refugees in charge of the neighborhoods and living tents to discuss the problem. Later she called for a meeting with only the women. All the women were on her side, and they found the solution: The man had to decide whether he would stay with her and the children in Colomoncagua, or go with the other woman to another camp. He decided to go with the other woman to another place despite the fact that he was the second coordinator of the camp. Afterwards the health worker was fine, and she felt very strong because of the support from the other women. From this and other episodes I learned a lot.

I learned that it is possible to live in a good and simple way, and that if there is a community, people can get along well with each other, and together seek solutions to their problems. I also learned that, yes, *machismo* is strong there, but the women are organizing in the midst of such a difficult situation.

I was accepted as a woman but looked upon differently because I was a foreigner. In reality, I lived like a man: I wasn't washing my own clothes, I didn't have any children, my life was completely oriented towards work which was not domestic. Whereas the refugee women had to do two things: They worked in the workshops and the health centers, and they also had to work in their tents. They often asked me about my life in Germany, because they wanted to know what the women did there.

Above all, it was important for them to know that they weren't alone, that there is a solidarity movement throughout the world and that there are foreigners who are ready to live with them and to support them in their efforts to change their situation.

For me, at the end of my work, the voices of the children remain in my memory, and images of the tents, the poverty, the work meetings.

But more than anything, what remains is the memory of the sadness, the happiness and the hope of the refugees, as when one of the children would die and they would be so sad, but at the same time they would try to look toward the future.

Returning home to Guajirla, Chalatenango after seven years in Honduran refugee camps (1987).

Reina Isabel

Reina Isabel Hernandes is a member of the directiva *of CRIPDES, the Christian Committee of the Displaced of El Salvador. This interview with her was conducted by New Americas Press in San Salvador in December 1986. Translation by New Americas Press.*

Returning Home (1986)

Could you tell us your name, and a little of your personal history?

My name is Reina Isabel. I am twenty-six years old and was born in a canton of the province of Cabañas. I grew up in the area where I was born. My family is a peasant family. They are considered rich peasants here in El Salvador, but they aren't really that rich. At the age of sixteen I started working with the Christian base community in my area. That's where my political experience and commitment to the people started. I was a catechist, and I helped prepare the children in our small village for communion. I also worked with a women's committee that we had in our parish called "Mary's Legion." At that time I worked with priests like Father Napoleón Macías. Some of them are now martyrs. Through my work with the base community, I learned something about the reality of our people.

How did your family feel about your work with the community?

They never objected, because, in spite of their good position in society, they understood the struggle of the people and didn't oppose it. They even suffered in the repression themselves. The repression really started in 1979. We had started to work with the popular organizations—like FECCAS (Christian Federation of Salvadoran Peasants) of the BPR (Revolutionary Popular Bloc)—when the government began to expel

233

priests and murder catechists, and threaten other people who worked in a religious way with the poor people in our village. My father and my uncles had worked with the popular organizations in our town. They had trucks and they used them to help people. So when the repression became bad, and so many *compañeros* were being killed, I fled with my family to Honduras. That was in 1980. I didn't want to go, but I was living with them and they insisted, so I left with them.

Did your mother go to Honduras as well?

I didn't grow up with my mother. I grew up with my grandparents. That's part of the story of my personal life. My mother is from a very poor family, and she was never married to my father. This is a common situation here in El Salvador. So when I was one, I'm told, my father's parents took me and I grew up with them. I did not get to meet my mother until I was grown-up, and now I don't even know where she lives. The last time I visited her was in 1978, and I haven't heard anything since. I just know that she lived around here in Sonsonate.

So I was with my grandparents in Honduras. At first they didn't want to live in the refugee camp, since they had been used to living in better conditions, and we got our own house in Honduras. But reports came from El Salvador that my family had collaborated with the guerrillas in the past, and then the Honduran army started persecuting us: Our house was burned down, our belongings were taken, everything. So in 1981 we went into the refugee camp of San Antonio, where I lived and worked for two years. As soon as I got there, I joined the refugee health unit, and once again I felt good, because I was working with my people. I earned the respect of many people, including people from other countries who worked at that camp. Many of the people who were in that camp are here now.

In 1983 I decided to come back to El Salvador. My family was against it, but I returned from Honduras to work with the people here. That year, I began to work with the Christian base communities of the displaced people in northern San Miguel. From there I also went to work with the displaced in Usulután Province. Most of my work has been with the communities of the displaced on the coast of Usulután. There are about six communities that I feel I am a part of, because I have shared in their lives and suffered the repression with them for over a year. The people of the coast of Usulután have suffered through many years of repression and misery, going from one place to the other, running and fleeing to and fro. That is why they decided to form a committee of the people who had been displaced.

After we had formed the committee, we started looking for ways to coordinate with the work of other displaced people in the country.

We heard that there was already a committee representing the displaced here in San Salvador. It was CRIPDES. We explained our situation to them, and the particular problems faced by the displaced communities on the coast. It was a difficult process, but we eventually succeeded in coordinating our work with CRIPDES. Then, in May of 1985, I was asked to come to San Salvador to work for CRIPDES and the displaced at a national level. I have been working with CRIPDES since that time. In May of 1986, a year later, a forum of the displaced was held and we decided to form the CNR (National Coordinating Committee for Repopulation) to implement the struggle for the return of the displaced to their places of origin.

Could you tell us about the work of CRIPDES and the CNR, and your role in them?

I usually work more with CRIPDES, but I've also had to work in the CNR because of the shortage of people. I don't have an official position in the CNR. I just work with the *compañeros,* doing whatever I can. But I am still a member of CRIPDES, and I am on the *directiva* of CRIPDES.

Since it was founded in 1984, CRIPDES has been the organization that represents the interests of the displaced here in El Salvador on a national level. CRIPDES brings together the displaced from different sectors, organizes them and, above all, motivates them to struggle to demand their rights.

As I said, the CNR arose from a forum called by CRIPDES in May 1986. The call for the forum came at a time when the large military operations were taking place, big operations like Operation Phoenix in Guazapa, where the army displaced more than 10,000 people, and Operation Carreño in Chalatenango, where thousands more peasants were rounded up. To deal with this crisis, we saw the need to form a committee of the displaced that could respond to these forced evictions with concrete actions. More than 500 delegates came together at the forum and decided to form the CNR. The goal of the CNR, as its name says, is to carry out the work of repopulation, resettling people back in their places of origin. CRIPDES and the CNR both work with the displaced, and coordinate together, but they have different functions. For instance, if CRIPDES is working in an area where there are families that want to be part of a resettlement, then CRIPDES will coordinate with the CNR. We tell them how many families want to go back, and then the CNR will coordinate the repopulation effort in that area. This is the relationship between CRIPDES and the CNR.

Our work at CRIPDES is broader because it organizes the displaced and helps them to understand their rights. Many people have been displaced because they are ignorant of their rights. Their houses were burned down, they lost everything and they were very afraid. But now they can see that it is to their advantage to organize, to struggle together, to get better living conditions—to have some work and a home life. They feel the government should pay them back for the destruction of their homes and their livestock. CRIPDES helps the displaced who are traumatized by their experiences, and are afraid of returning to their homes, but want to work to improve the difficult living conditions where they are settled now. With these people, CRIPDES works to promote literacy, to form workshops and to provide food. This is an important part of our work.

What has the CNR achieved during the past year, and what are the hopes for the new year?

The goal of the CNR since its creation has been to resettle those who have been evicted from their homes, to take them back so they can begin again and work again on their land. The displaced here in the city live in refugee "slums." They are unable to work freely. Most of us are peasants and, well, the peasant only knows how to work the land. Life in the city is hard for us. So the main objective for this past year has been to bring some of the displaced back to their land, and we feel we have achieved this. San José las Flores in Chalatenango has been resettled, as has El Barillo, in Cuscatlán. Even though some of the living conditions in these communities are still very difficult, the people are so happy to be back on their land. There is a shortage of food, and very few social services. The Salvadoran army often keeps the people from leaving to get supplies in town, and stops medicines and food from coming in to the communities. But we believe that people's living conditions are better now than in the refugee camps, and we see these two resettlements as a major accomplishment.

Now the government wants to take advantage of what the displaced have done and says that it permits these resettlements because of the "new democratic system." But if we had waited for Duarte to say, "Yes, you can return to San José las Flores," the people would still be in refugee camps. But we said, "We are Salvadorans, this is our homeland, and we have the right to live wherever we want." So these achievements come from the unity of our struggle and not because Duarte's government is improving the democratic system and respecting human rights. Therefore, for 1987, and for the duration of the conflict, our struggle has to be continuous—for respect of human rights, for the rights of the displaced and for an end to evictions. For the CNR, the work will not end until all the displaced, all the refugees, inside and outside of the country, have returned to their places of origin.

Could you tell us what happened in the attempt to repopulate San Carlos Lempa?

The case of San Carlos Lempa was different from that of San José las Flores. The displaced that arrived at San Carlos Lempa were not an organized group. They were people who had suddenly left an area of conflict because they couldn't stand the bombing, machine-gunning and big military operations. This was in the areas of San Vicente volcano and Tecoluca. These people got together and decided to repopulate San Carlos Lempa. As soon as they had arrived there, they sent a delegation to San Salvador to let it be known that they had been evicted from their homes, and that they would be staying in San Carlos Lempa. The CNR formed a delegation to visit the people there and called a press conference to ask that the rights of these people be respected. Before these actions by the CNR, they had been alone, without support or material help—they only had some nylon tarps to set up for shelter.

Of course the army took advantage of this situation. They accused the people at San Carlos of being FMLN *masas* [masses, or sympathizers], who had gotten tired of fleeing. The army then removed them by force from San Carlos Lempa. Of course, the army manipulated the whole thing. COPREFA (the Salvadoran Army Press Corps) said that eighty-one FMLN supporters had been "rescued." They made it sound like they were protecting the people instead of capturing them. But in reality, the army did not want the people to remain in San Carlos Lempa. Instead, they wanted to make them part of their United to Reconstruct plan,[6] and they took them away and held them. We demanded that the army take the people to the Archbishop in San Salvador. After a month and a half, the army agreed to do this, and tried to claim that they were respecting human rights. But San Carlos Lempa is still not repopulated.

What is the relationship between the organizations of the displaced— CNR and CRIPDES—and the other sectors of the popular movement?

The Salvadoran struggle is a process that has been developing little by little. In 1986 we made many positive steps in uniting the many different sectors of peasants, workers, students, displaced and relatives of political prisoners to work together towards the same objectives.

One of the positive steps of 1986 was the formation of the UNTS (National Unity of Salvadoran Workers), which represents the struggle of all Salvadorans—that is, the working people, the poor people. We as the displaced know that our main task is to carry out the struggle to return to our places of origin, and to demand housing and respect for our human rights. But there's a saying, "One finger doesn't make a hand." Therefore, if all the sectors unite, we will all have strength. In the assembly of the UNTS in November 1986, agreements were made with special points for each sector of the popular movement. These included support for the return of the displaced to their places of origin, to wherever they want to live. We believe that one person's pain and sorrow is the pain and sorrow of all—for we are convinced that one person's struggle is the struggle of all.

Will the repopulations you're planning for the future be done with the help of international volunteers?

Yes, we consider an international presence very important, because it assures the people that they are not alone and that if there is any trouble, it can be minimized. If the army is repressive, it will have greater consequences internationally. During the repopulation of El Barillo, the security forces at Aguacayo detained and deported the twenty-three foreigners who were accompanying the repopulation. This had a negative effect on Duarte's political position, his prestige and respect internationally. We feel that the presence of the international delegations is very important, even though the people themselves have to be very conscious and prepared for whatever problems might arise.

What is your opinion of women's role in the process, and have you seen it changing over the years you've been involved in the struggle?

The role of women has definitely been developing within the struggle of the Salvadoran people. As I told you, when I worked as a catechist in the ecclesiastic groups, I was part of a women's group that we called "Mary's Legion." One of the things we did was to meet and discuss the condition of women, our oppression due to *machismo,* and so on. We began to see that we are equal to men, and that we should have the same rights and opportunities, because we can do any job that men do.

We feel that we are developing an important role as women within the struggle of our country, which includes struggling to change that system of marginalization, that double oppression we women suffer from. Because on top of suffering at the hands of the rich oligarchy, we also suffer as women. That's why we call it double oppression, and that is why we struggle.

There are many men involved in the struggle who understand this. Of course, sometimes there are clashes, because some people still do not understand. But many of the *compañeros* have acquired this new thinking and, based on that, I already feel liberated from the feeling of inferiority, which most women in this country still experience. They feel they are less than the men. A woman will get married, work hard for the man, care for the children, and feel like she cannot participate in a committee. Or if she's on a committee, she feels she has to get her husband's permission for everything. She does not believe she can do anything without feeling tied to a man, who dominates her. Well, I don't feel that way. I feel that I am free and am capable of deciding my life for myself. I feel secure in what I do, and I'm not dependent on someone else. Nor do I feel marginalized by a bunch of men. I think that perhaps this whole struggle has helped women to gain knowledge of how to contribute, and how to liberate ourselves from the traditional thinking.

Is there a difference between how you felt six years ago and now?

Well, of course. Six years ago I worked with the people, but I didn't feel the same independence. When I fled to Honduras, I felt tied down, dominated, that there was someone else deciding things for me. Now I feel certain of what I do and why I do it, and that's a difference that's come through the process of struggle for the people.

When we were in El Barillo, we noticed that there were no women on the directiva *there. Why is that?*

When the cooperative was formed in El Barillo, the people decided not to put a woman on the *directiva*, even though many women are carrying out important work there. There are still many women who are fully committed to the work of raising their children, working in their households, and who are less incorporated into the community work. But other women are very involved. For instance, there is a committee of women who are responsible for the vegetable garden which produces food for the whole community. Even though there are no women on the *directiva*,[7] there are still women working to support the community. And although equal participation has not been reached in places like El Barillo, there have been positive changes in women's participation in the work. Within CRIPDES and the CNR, there are many women on the *directivas*, and that says a lot. The other day someone asked me, "Are there men in CRIPDES, or only women?" "No," I answered, "there are both men and women, but on the *directivas* of both CRIPDES and the CNR, the majority are women."

"Our Will To Continue Has Not Been Broken" (1989)

On April 19, 1989, Reina Isabel Hernandes was one of seventy people detained by the Hacienda (Treasury) Police during a raid on the CRIPDES office. Following are excerpts from Isabel's testimony, recorded in Ilopango prison by the non-governmental Commission on Human Rights (CDHES) on May 2.

At 3:15 p.m., our office was surrounded by the Hacienda Police. Without explanation, they banged on the doors and demanded that we open them. We refused, knowing that their aim was to capture us and burglarize the office, and then accuse us of being a "front" organization... At 4:30 p.m., a contingent of anti-riot police came in as reinforcements, forming a barrier in front of the entrance to prevent journalists or humanitarian organizations from getting in... At 11:30 p.m. they forced their way into the office and pushed us all into one room. Then they took us out, one by one, loaded us onto a military truck...and took us to the headquarters of the Hacienda Police.

For the next thirty-six hours, Isabel was repeatedly interrogated and tortured, as her captors "questionned" her about CRIPDES and accused her of recruiting for the FMLN. She repeatedly denied their charges of FMLN ties while maintaining the legitimacy of her work at CRIPDES. During this period she was kept standing and blindfolded; she was also denied food and water, and was not allowed to use a bathroom.

...As part of the interrogation they brought in a man who said he knew me, that he was part of my family... He said that we had been in school together, and that he knew the priest who had organized me because he had been in the same meetings. They took off the blindfold so I could see him, but I didn't recognize him, or remember ever having seen him.

...They continued the interrogation, and with each question I was hit on the head or in the back. When I fell to the floor the torturer said, "Who told you you could fall?" He kicked me or pulled my hair to get me back up. Because it was so hot and I had not eaten, I was very thirsty and had bad pains in my stomach. But when I asked for water, they said I wouldn't get any until I agreed to their accusations.

...Early Thursday morning they stopped interrogating me for two hours and left me standing in front of a wall. When I could no longer support myself, I leaned against the wall. When the guard saw me do this, he beat me and forced me to stand again. I felt very faint...I had not slept for two nights, or had anything to eat or drink. I also had cramps from arthritis and a terrible headache from the constant beatings, as well as from the screams of the other *compañeros* being tortured.

...Near dawn on Friday they came for me again, for the fifth time, and took me to another interrogation room... Three men came in, including the one who claimed to be my cousin, and beat me. After they left, another man put some music on a tape deck, which made my head pound even more. He continued interrogating me and told me, "Don't you understand? If you don't tell the truth, you are going to die here." Then he knocked me to the floor with a single blow... He handcuffed me so that my hands were behind my back and tied a rubber hood over my head and threw me onto the floor. There was lime in the bag and I almost suffocated. He took the hood off until I came to, then put it on again and threw me back on the ground, even harder than before... He put the hood back over my head a fifth time, and pulled me up by my hair and my hands, which were still handcuffed behind me. Then some other men kneed me in the thorax and beat me on the base of my spine. They dropped me again and I fainted. When I came to, they kicked at me to get up, but I fell down again, and my whole body was shaking.

He was about to put on the rubber hood and hang me by my wrists again, but I couldn't take anymore, so I told him that I would accept the charges they were making... I was more dead than alive, and so when he said, "You have been with the FPL since 1980," I only answered, "Yes." He continued reading the statement they had made up, and I only answered, "Yes." Then they took me to the bathroom, threw water on me and left me sitting against a wall. Each man that passed by kicked me or punched me in the head.

Later that day, Friday, April 21, Reina Isabel and six other women who had also been captured on April 19 were taken before a judge, where the declarations they had signed under extreme duress were read. Three other men from the CRIPDES directiva who had been captured at the same time were also in court. The women were transferred to Ilopango Prison. On April 25, Isabel and the two other detained women members of the CRIPDES directiva issued a statement to their supporters. The following is an excerpt from that statement, as translated by the Committee in Solidarity with the People of El Salvador (CISPES), Washington, D.C.

...The main goal of the repression against us is to destroy the popular organizations by terrorizing their members and leaders, and to prevent them from fighting for their just demands. As women and displaced people who have lived with the effects of the war for the past eight years, we want to make it clear to our brothers and sisters in solidarity that, despite the torture inflicted on us by the Treasury Police and our continuing incarceration, our will to continue fighting for the rights of the displaced—and all our people—has not been broken.

... We thank all of you who have acted in solidarity to demand our freedom... They have deprived us of our liberty, but not our love of peace, justice and freedom, and we are sure that we will very soon return to join the struggle of our people, the displaced of El Salvador.

In spite of the detention of half its leadership, the theft of the food supplies being gathered for displaced communities and the destruction of its office, CRIPDES quickly resumed its work with the displaced around the country. The committee was also able to mobilize thousands of the displaced to the annual May 1 workers' march in San Salvador, to demonstrate their continuing determination to win their rights, as well as the release of their leaders. In addition, Isabel and the other prisoners from the April 19 raids immediately revived COPPES (Political Prisoners of El Salvador) to demand medical attention for their injuries, decent food, mattresses and outside visits. Most of their demands have been met.

Notes

Preface

1. MADRE is a New York-based nonprofit organization dedicated to developing political and material support for the women of Nicaragua and El Salvador.

2. The North American Congress on Latin America (NACLA) publishes the bimonthly *Report on the Americas* and sponsors research on political, economic and social developments in Latin America and the Caribbean.

Introduction

1. AMES, "Reflections of Salvadoran Women," *Monthly Review,* New York, June 1982

2. Thomas P. Anderson, *Matanza: El Salvador's Communist Revolt of 1932,* Lincoln, NE: University of Nebraska Press, 1971.

Part I

1. From "Women and Human Rights in El Salvador," by the Organizing Committee for the First Encounter of Salvadoran Women, September 1988.

2. From "The Position and Role of Women in the Current Situation in El Salvador," by ASIPES, CREFAC and ASPS, San Salvador, September 1988.

3. From "Health and Society," by Carlos A. Lopez, Program of Health Sciences, CSUCA, San Salvador, 1983.

4. Women's participation in the UNTS has increased significantly since the time of this interview. Over one-half of the 650 delegates to the UNTS's National Congress in October 1988 were women.

Part III

1. *No Me Agarran Viva,* Claribel Alegría (Mexico City: Ediciones Era, 1983). *They Won't Take Me Alive,* Claribel Alegría, (Amanda Hopkinson, translator) (London: Women's Press, Ltd., 1987).

Part IV

1. According to a report by the Interfaith Office on Accompaniment in Washington, D.C., there was, on average, one military incursion per week against the town of Arcatao in the six months following October 1987. On December 10, 1987, two weeks after this interview was conducted, Salvadoran army troops invaded Arcatao, occupying houses and firing weapons indiscriminately for two straight days. On March 23, 1988, the Salvadoran air force bombed and strafed the town, killing two residents who were in their fields planting crops. On other occasions women have been raped and fields around the town mined by the military. In addition, 95 percent of Arcatao's food crops in 1988 were destroyed by government forces.

2. The Esquipulas II Peace Accords, signed by the five Central American presidents in August 1987, include a provision calling on the signatories to allow and facilitate the unimpeded return of refugees to their homes.

Part V

1. On May 14, 1980, 600 Salvadoran peasants were killed by Salvadoran and Honduran troops. Many of the victims were shot as they tried to cross the Sumpul River into Honduras, to escape a Salvadoran army offensive. On March 17, 1981, seventy people—primarily women and children—were murdered by the Salvadoran army as they tried to ford the Lempa River into Honduras. Another massacre occurred at the Sumpul River on May 30, 1982, as 2,000 peasants were attacked by helicopters and mortar fire while trying to cross the river; over 200 were killed on that day.

2. The Sanctuary Movement is a large network of U.S. religious congregations that provide shelter and other assistance to Salvadoran and Guatemalan refugees fleeing repression in their countries. Since its beginnings in 1982, the Sanctuary Movement has been an important force in bringing the plight of Central American refugees to the attention of the North American public.

3. "The Fourteen Families" is what Salvadorans call the tiny oligarchy that has traditionally controlled most of El Salvador's land and wealth.

4. In 1983, the UN High Commission on Refugees proposed a plan, sponsored by the U.S. and Honduran governments, to move the refugees from the camps near the border to new camps deeper inside Honduras (to Olanchito, in

The El Salvadoran women's struggles connected include the struggles of their families of repression. Race + class + imperalism

northeastern Honduras). The refugees adamantly refused to be relocated, and the plan was eventually dropped.

5. La Virtud is a small border village where many of the refugees first settled on entering Honduras in 1980 and 1981. Most of the refugees in La Virtud were involuntarily relocated to Mesa Grande (fifty kilometers from the border) in early 1982.

6. United to Reconstruct, initiated in July 1986, was a plan devised by U.S. advisers to dislodge the FMLN from its areas of support and to consolidate popular support for the government. In theory, the army would drive out the guerrillas, and then the government would institute community reconstruction projects and other civic action programs, such as civil defense units. In practice, United to Reconstruct operated under the complete control of the military and amounted to little more than a new name for the army's ongoing counterinsurgency war against the FMLN and its civilian support base.

7. By the fall of 1988 there were at least two women on the El Barillo *directiva*.

Background of the women.
nature of the organizations
objectives + goals.
commonalities with other third world women we have read about.
commonalities with the 1st world women.

role of the church) in the
role of the state } lives of
role of the US.) these women

How are they similar or different from woman at pt zero?
Male-female relations structure of the family.

About New Americas Press

New Americas Press (formerly Solidarity Publications) is a San Francisco-based small press collective founded in 1980 to produce and distribute educational materials from the perspective of Central Americans in struggle for social justice, national sovereignty and peace. The goal of the Press is to inform people about the effects of U.S. policy in Central America and promote understanding of the causes of the conflicts in the region, through materials embodying the words and aspirations of the people of Central America. *A Dream Compels Us* is the result of a project initiated by the Press in 1984, in response to a suggestion by representatives of the Women's Association of El Salvador (AMES).

After ten years of producing materials in solidarity with the people of Central America, New Americas Press will close at the end of 1989, due to a chronic shortage of resources and the commitment of collective members to other solidarity projects. The collective has requested that royalties from the sale of *A Dream Compels Us* be donated to the following organizations, in support of their projects that directly benefit the women of El Salvador. Readers are encouraged to offer their support through these organizations as well.

- NEST Foundation (PO Box 411436, San Francisco, CA 94141, 415-864-7755) supports leadership training for women in the marginalized communities of San Salvador, and women's production workshops in displaced communities in the countryside.

- MADRE (121 West 27th Street, #301, New York, NY 10001, 212-627-0444) currently funds the women's health and hygiene project of the Union of Salvadoran Women and is working on setting up a children's clinic in a marginalized community outside of San Salvador.

About South End Press

South End Press is a nonprofit, collectively run book publisher with over 150 titles in print. Since our founding in 1977, we have tried to meet the needs of readers who are exploring or are already committed to the politics of radical social change. Our goal is to publish books that encourage critical thinking and constructive action on the key political, cultural, social, economic and ecological issues shaping life in the United States and in the world. In this way, we hope to give expression to a wide diversity of democratic social movements and to provide an alternative to the products of corporate publishing.

If you would like to receive a free catalog of South End Press books or get information on our membership program—which, for $40, offers two free books and a 40% discount on all titles—please write us at South End Press, 116 St. Botolph Street, Boston, MA 02115.

Other Books of Interest Available from South End Press

Roots of Rebellion: Land and Hunger in Central America
Tom Barry

Gift of the Devil: A History of Guatemala
Jim Handy

The Caribbean, 1989 Updated Edition
Catherine Sunshine

Turning the Tide: U.S. Intervention in Central America and the Struggle for Peace
Noam Chomsky

Washington's War on Nicaragua
Holly Sklar

Mothers of the Disappeared
Jo Fisher

Honduras: The Making of a Banana Republic
Alison Acker

El Salvador, The Face of Revolution
Robert Armstrong and Janet Shenk

248